Caldwell
56 Vicar's Hill
S E 13.

PLEASURE WITH PAPER

by the same author

*

ADVENTURES WITH PAPER

PLEASURE
WITH PAPER

by

A. VAN BREDA

Translated by W. E. JAMES

Introduction by

ANTONIA RIDGE

FABER AND FABER LIMITED

24 Russell Square

London

First published in England in mcmliv
by Faber and Faber Limited
24 Russell Square London W.C.1
Printed in Great Britain by
Latimer Trend & Co Ltd Plymouth
All rights reserved

This book was originally published as
PLEZIER MET PAPIER by Uitgeverij
van Breda, Amsterdam, Holland.

INTRODUCTION

This is a book from Holland, but it will delight children of all ages everywhere—for every right-minded child the world over loves to use his hands and *make things*.

Here is page after page of interesting, useful and amusing models, all within the reach of any child who is prepared to remember two points:

1. It is necessary to have patience as well as a pair of scissors, paper, paste and a pencil.
2. It really pays to read directions carefully. This definitely saves time and temper as well as paper.

My brother translated this book, but he and I spent many a happy hour making every model in turn. We both feel that the title of this book tells nothing but the truth—from cover to cover it is full of 'Pleasure with Paper'.

ANTONIA RIDGE

CONTENTS

FOREWORD

As I write this Foreword for *Pleasure with Paper* there lies around me a whole world of paper—paper animals, paper dolls, paper sledges, barrows, masks and fancy decorations—the result of months of cutting out, folding and sticking together, and seeking something fresh from which children might derive pleasure.

To be honest, working with paper quite got me in its grip. Well-known things are given in this book as well as new ones. The longer I make drawings, cut out paper, fold and paste it, the more convinced I become of the tremendous possibilities that lie in a simple piece of paper. The scope is practically unlimited. If the work is taken up in the right manner and with imagination, vistas will open which children will, sooner or later, want to explore further for themselves, particularly if they are encouraged in the first instance by parents or teachers.

Paper is cheap and easy to obtain. The only other things children will want are confined to a pencil, a good pair of scissors, a pot of paste, a ruler, a tube or two of paint or box of water-colours. For some things a compass will be of help. These are all things usually found in a household where there are school children. Everything is easy to handle, and, with this book before them, children can start straight away. In less than no time the room will be full of fancy chains. Tables and chairs will be bright with decorative cloths and centres.

On the floor will range a whole zoo of animals. The children will disguise themselves in paper masks. They will endeavour to fox you all with their 'Magic Paper Rings' or ask if you can solve the problem of the 'Wellington Boots'. I certainly hope they will be able to interest you; and that, in fact, you yourself will soon be reaching for the scissors in order to join the children in their fun.

It seems hardly necessary for me to stress the educational value of this work, pleasurable though it is. My primary purpose in producing this book was to set forth ideas which would stimulate children to busy themselves interestingly and profitably in making things in an inexpensive manner. I naturally also nurture the hope that it will lead to a better appreciation of handicraft all round.

May this book give much pleasure!

v. B.

USEFUL RULES
(Please do read them before you begin)

MATERIALS

Paper. You will be told the best kind of paper to use for each model. There are, of course, many kinds of paper—plain or coloured paper which lends itself to folding (paper traders call this sort *Bank* paper), tinted paper or paper highly coloured on one side (trade name is *Flint*), strong paper or drawing paper (*Cartridge*), black paper (*Silhouette*), or thicker material still, such as cardboard (*Three-sheet Board*) about the same thickness as a postcard. You can buy all these in the shops. For trying out and practising there is always a lot of paper in your own home that can be used up: newspapers, magazines, brown paper, odd strips of wallpaper—even old letters (but if you want to cut these up be sure to ask first).

Scissors. Any ordinary pair of household scissors will do, provided they are reasonably sharp.

Paste. Some people like to make up their own from crystals, powders, flour, or dextrine. It is often more convenient to buy ready-made paste or gum in little pots. Do not use too much at a time, and *always* put the lid or cover back on when you have finished.

Colouring. Your finished models can, of course, be greatly improved by colouring. Chalks are not advised, because the colours rub off so easily. Coloured pencils are much better, both for the models and your hands. Provided you are fairly good at it, painting with water-colours gives by far the best results. Decorate sparingly though, as too much water tends to crinkle your model out of shape.

Pencil, Ruler, Compass. You *must* have a pencil and a ruler marked in centimetres. When you come to make such things as Merry-go-Rounds you will also need a compass. Avoid ruling heavy lines.

METHOD OF WORKING

The drawings will show you how to set about each step in making your model, *so look before you cut.* Once you have understood how to make a model you can then start improving on it in any way you like. Please use your ruler carefully if a measurement is given; otherwise your figure will not work out properly. For most models you will have to use a piece of paper folded in two. Sometimes several pieces of paper have to be folded and folded more than once. Study the drawings and note carefully where the crease comes. In some cases it is at the top; in others it may be at the bottom, or to the left or right. Below are four drawings which should make the method of working clear.

 a   *b*   *c*   *d*

(*a*) Fold a piece of paper in two with the crease at the top.
(*b*) Draw with your pencil the figure of the animal as shown

above and then with your scissors cut it out. (Never cut along the line of the crease.)

(*c*) Now your cut-out object should look like *c*.

(*d*) The remaining portion of your piece of paper will look like *d*.

MOST IMPORTANT

Looking through the book, you will probably like some models more than others and be eager to try them out, but more than likely these will prove to be the most difficult ones. It is best to begin at the beginning of the book and to work steadily through it patiently and accurately, gaining more and more skill with each model you make.

FESTIVE CHAINS

These Chains are very easy to make. All you need are strips of coloured paper, the more brightly-coloured the better. You can get yards and yards of lovely decorations from very little material.

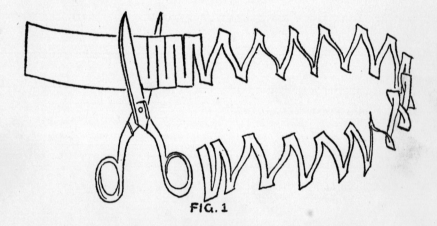

FIG. 1

Fig. 1. Take a strip of coloured paper and cut slits in it up and down, like this. Do this all the way along the strip. Then gently pull the strip out from both ends.

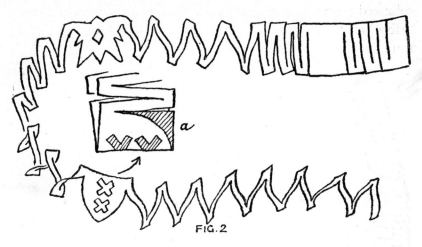

FIG. 2

Fig. 2. Make this Chain in the same way, except that every now and then you leave a square portion of the paper uncut. Fold one of these squares in two. Cut out the shaded parts shown in *a.* Unfold your square, and you get a Coat of Arms. Fold and cut bits out of other squares and see what fancy shapes you yourself can make.

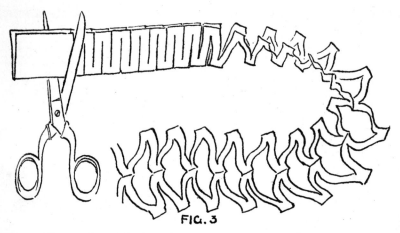

FIG. 3

Fig. 3. To make this Double Chain, first fold your strip of coloured paper in two, longways. Make slits up and down as before, and then unfold your paper. Now pull the Chain out from both ends.

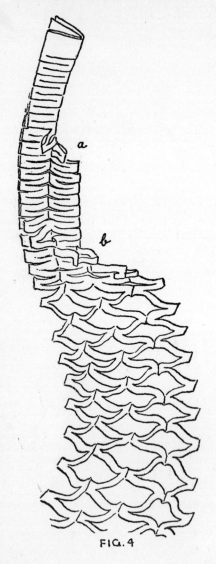

FIG. 4

Fig. 4. For this Chain you need a wider strip of coloured paper. Fold it in two longways. Do this *twice*. Cut up and down slits as before. Unfold your paper carefully on the table, remembering that there are two folds to undo. Now (and only now) pull out the strip at both ends. You then get the splendid Christmas decoration shown below *b.*

If you want to decorate a large room quickly, lay four or five strips on top of one another. With sharp scissors you can cut them all out in one go.

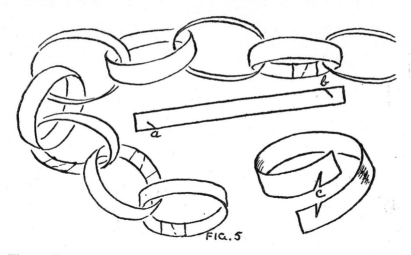

Fig. 5. For this Chain you need strips of thick paper. At the ends of each strip make sloping cuts, as at *a* and *b*. These cuts must make slits exactly half the width of the paper. Make your first ring by curving the ends of a strip round and fitting the slits together. (Take a look at *c*.) Now put your next strip through your first ring and again join the ends together. Keep on linking strips in this way, until you have as long a Chain as you want.

Fig. 6. This Chain is made in the same way, only you need somewhat wider strips of paper than before. First fold each strip, as at *a*. Next fold again, as at *b*. Now draw with your pencil and ruler a pattern, as in *b*.

Cut the folded paper along your pencilled lines, unfold your strip fully, and you get *c*. Make half-way sloping slits at both ends—just as you did in Fig. 5, to fasten the ends of your ring.

At *d* is drawn a grander kind of decorative ring. Why not try to make this too?

When linking your rings together you can vary your chains. If you like you can join large rings to small, plain ones to fancy ones, and so on.

FIG. 6

JACOB'S LADDER

Fig. 1. Take a strip of paper, not too thick—ordinary newspaper would do. It must be ten times longer than it is wide. A piece 12 × 120 cm. (centimetres) is a good size. Roll it into a tube, like this, but take care that the hole within the tube is about 1½ cm. across. To prevent your tube unrolling, brush a little paste on the end of your strip, and stick it well down.

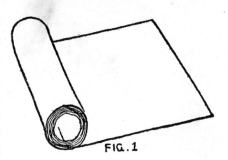

FIG. 1

Fig. 2. Cut out half the tube, like this, except for the portions at both ends.

FIG. 2

Fig. 3. Press the whole thing flat on the table, so that it looks like this.

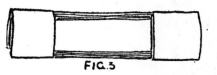

FIG. 3

Fig. 4. Bend both ends downwards.

FIG. 4

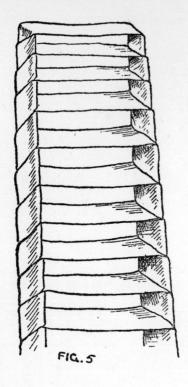

FIG. 5

Fig. 5. Take both the turned-down ends in one hand, and, with the other hand, carefully pull up the top layer of the flat portion. *Don't pull it up too much.* Next pull the second layer carefully upwards. Now the third layer, and so on. These are the steps of the ladder. Keep pulling up steps until the whole ladder is out, then neatly straighten out the side pieces.

CHRISTMAS TREE

Fig. 1. Using thin paper (ordinary newspaper will do), make a tube, as you did for the Jacob's Ladder. Make six long cuts in the tube, all the same length, nearly to the end, like this.

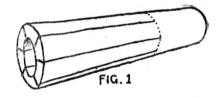

FIG. 1

Fig. 2. Flatten down the six equal cut portions, like this. The lower part is then the trunk of your tree.

FIG. 2

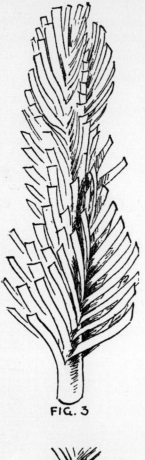

FIG. 3

Fig. 3. Take the trunk in one hand. With the other hand carefully separate and draw up the *top* layer of each of the six flattened portions. Then draw the next layer. Keep doing this with each layer until the tree looks like this.

FIG. 4

Fig. 4. To get the tree to stand up on its own, make four snips upwards at the bottom of the trunk. Bend the four cut portions out-wards, like this. Now you can stick them on to a piece of cardboard and your Christmas Tree will not topple over.

26

PALM TREE

For this you need two strips of thin coloured paper; a broad *green* strip measuring about 12 × 50 cm.; and a narrower *brown* strip measuring about 6 × 50 cm. These two colours will make your Palm Tree look quite real.

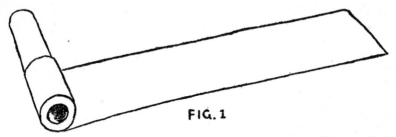

FIG. 1

Fig. 1. Make a tube of the green paper, and in rolling it leave a hole inside of about 1 cm. across. Round the bottom half of the tube paste a layer or two of the brown strip. Next roll the rest of the brown strip round the green tube.

Fig. 2. For the time being—to prevent any unrolling—fasten a paper clip in the bottom, holding both rolls, like this. Make three cuts in the part of the green roll which still shows, dividing it into three equal portions.

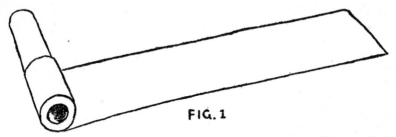

FIG. 2

Fig. 3. Trim the ends of each of the three parts, like this.

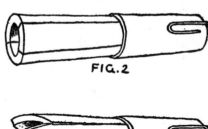

FIG. 3

Fig. 4. Cut tiny snips all round the green edges, as shown. This will give your palm leaves a feathery effect.

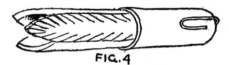

FIG. 4

27

FIG. 5

Fig. 5. Now flatten down the three green portions, like this.

FIG. 6

Fig. 6. Take away the paper clip, but hold the bottom of your tree, so that it doesn't unroll. Gently pull the trunk of the palm tree upwards. When it is tall enough, put a lick of gum on the loose end —where you had your paper clip—and stick it down. Now the layers of leaves have to be separated and made to look like this. Wiggle them about with your little finger.

The Palm Tree can be made to stand up on its own in the same way as the Christmas Tree. (Take a look at Fig. 4 again on page 26.)

28

PARTY TRICK

How to Get your Head through a Post Card

Fig. 1. Take a plain post card or a piece of cardboard of same shape. Fold it longways so that the crease comes at the top, like this. Now cut slits, first from the top and then from the bottom, as you did when making your festive chains (Fig. 3 on page 19). Unfold your post card and cut along the line of the crease, but only from slit A to slit B. (Take a good look at the drawing.) You *don't* cut the post card at the far ends.

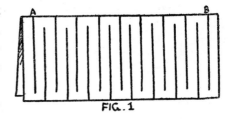

FIG. 1

Fig. 2. Gently pull out the ends. Now you will be able to get your head right through the post card, like this. It is all a case of 'knowing how'.

FIG. 2

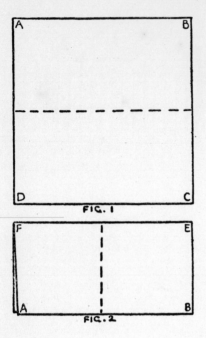

FIG. 1

Fig. 1. Take a square of stiff, strong paper, measuring about 20 × 20 cm. Fold it in two, so that edge AB falls exactly on edge DC.

FIG. 2

Fig. 2. Fold it again in two, so that edges AF fall on edges BE.

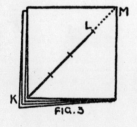

FIG. 3

Fig. 3. Measure the distance from K to M. (If it helps, draw a faint line from K to M.) Make a special mark at L three-quarters of the way up KM. Now cut through all pieces along the line from K to L.

Fig. 4. Unfold and flatten out your square. Bring the top point of each of the four cut parts to the centre of the square, like this. Now stick a big strong pin through the four points and the centre itself. (The bigger the head of the pin, the better.)

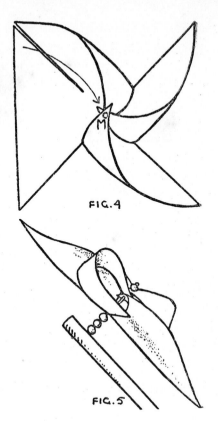

FIG. 4

Fig. 5. Next, you will want, of course, to put your Windmill on a stick. Before you do this, slip a few beads on the pin, like this. Then tap the pin firmly into your stick. Now you can take your Windmill out into the open and see it turn in the wind.

FIG. 5

CUTTING OUT

Before starting these, read once more the General Rules on pages 15 to 17. For the things you are now going to make thin coloured paper, or paper coloured or tinted one side and gummed at the back, will serve your purpose. When you have progressed sufficiently to cut out shapes without first drawing the design, you can use special black 'Silhouette' paper, which is very effective for this sort of work. One disadvantage

31

of black paper is, of course, that you cannot easily draw out-lines on it.

In each case you commence by folding your paper in two, so that the crease comes on the left side, as below. On the top layer or fold of your paper you first draw the half of whatever shape you are going to make. Then, by cutting along your pencilled lines, you get, when you unfold your paper, two joined halves which you smooth gently out. The complete shape is often most surprising. Work through the examples given below, and soon you will be making even more astonishingly clever things on your own. You must take care not to cut up or along the crease or fold itself.

Small sharp-pointed scissors are best for this work. When you have practised a lot and feel confident, try cutting out a design from plain folded paper *without* first doing a drawing. Don't be discouraged if the first few attempts turn out badly. Keep trying. You will quickly become quite expert; and then you can turn to using the black 'Silhouette' paper. This gives really wonderful results.

Silhouettes look best when they are pasted on cardboard of another colour. Brush paste thinly all over the cardboard. Lay your Silhouette on it and carefully smooth the Silhouette flat. Surplus paste can afterwards be dried off with blotting paper.

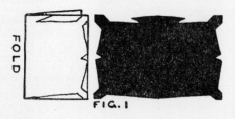

FOLD

FIG. 1

Fig. 1. Labels, Tags, Tabs. Draw any sort of design you like on your folded paper. Cut along the lines you have drawn. Push unwanted pieces aside, and unfold your Label.

By folding two or three pieces of paper at a time, you can make lots of Labels, Tags, or Tabs, in one go.

Fig. 2. Leaves. This drawing gives you just *one* example of a leaf. You can, of course, copy any leaf you like. There are lots of different sorts of leaves.

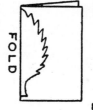

FIG. 2

Fig. 3. Butterflies. A little more difficult, but once you have cut out this one, you will want to copy other types of beautiful butterflies.

FIG. 3

Fig. 4. Kettle. Here are a couple of new useful tricks. Draw and cut out the kettle, as shown. Now cut out the shaded part, too—this makes the handle. Next, unfold your paper and cut off *one* of the spouts. (Try your hand at a Teapot!)

FIG. 4

Fig. 5. A Little Man. Draw and cut out in exactly the same way as before. When you unfold, you will laugh to see your shape with two

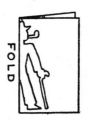 

FIG. 5

C

pipes in his mouth and two walking sticks. You cut one pipe off, and—on the other side—cut off one walking stick. (Try to do a lady with an umbrella.)

Fig. 6. Fencers. This is a tricky one to do, but it shows you how to tackle even more difficult designs and get better and better results. (Try boxers, dancers, knights jousting.)

FIG. 6

Figs. 7–8. Flower Pot. This looks more difficult than it really is. Try it out, and you will be surprised what good results you get—even at the first go. By using coloured paper and pasting your shapes on other material you can make your own Christmas Cards, Birthday Cards, Greetings Cards, Menu Cards. What a lot of money you'll be able to save!

FIG 7

FIG. 8

Fig. 9. Two Acrobats. Here is another useful trick. First fold your paper as before. Now fold it again downwards, so that the crease is at the top. Draw the figure, like this. Cut out, and carefully unfold.

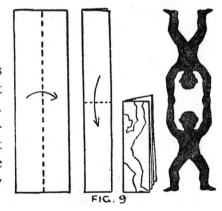

FIG. 9

35

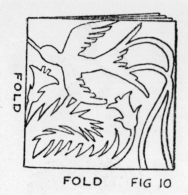

FOLD   **FIG 10**

Figs. 10–11. Birds and Flowers. Fold the paper *twice*, as for the Acrobats. This is just another example of what *can* be done.

FIG. 11

36

A FARM-HOUSE

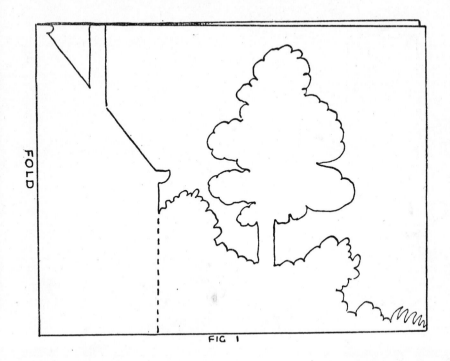

FIG 1

Fig. 1. Take thick paper, like drawing paper, and fold it in two with the crease on the left, as above. The same size as this will do. Draw the outlines, and cut away the unwanted portions. Unfold, flatten, and smooth out the crease. Cut off one chimney. Draw a door and windows, as in Fig. 7, on page 40. Cut the door so that it opens. Cut windows to open too, if you like. Now bend the shape both sides along the dotted line above, so that your house stands up on its own.

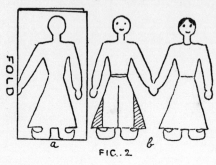

FIG. 2

Fig. 2. *Farmer and His Wife.* Fold a piece of paper in two so that the crease is on the left side, as at *a*. Draw a picture like that also shown at *a*. Cut out and unfold. You now have two farmer's wives. From one cut off the shaded portions of the skirt —see *b*. This will make the farmer. With your pencil draw eyes and noses, and, lower down, belts. Next, cut a slit up the farmer to make his legs, and separate them so that one foot comes forward and the other backward a bit. Both figures will now stand on their own, hand in hand.

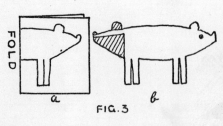

FIG. 3

Fig. 3. *A Pig.* Fold a piece of paper, with the crease at the left. Draw a picture as at *a*. Cut out and unfold. This gives you a funny two-headed pig, until you cut off the shaded portions shown in *b*. Make slits up for legs and pull them apart a bit. Draw an eye on each side. Twist the tail so that it curls up.

Fig. 4. A Cow. This is made in the same way as the pig.

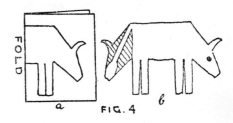

FIG. 4

Fig. 5. A Rabbit. Also made in exactly the same way. After slitting up and pulling apart the legs, bend them forward as at *c*.

FIG. 5

Fig. 6. Geese. Fold a piece of paper *four* times as at *a*. Draw a goose and cut out. Unfold and cut off *every other* goose, making a line of four geese as at *b*. Bend the bottom border, and your geese will stand on their own.

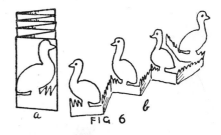

FIG 6

39

FIG. 7

Fig. 7. Here is the farmyard. You can either colour it all yourself with coloured pencils or paints, *or* make it from paper of different colours, just as you like. You can also add to your farm by making such things as barns, haystacks, chicken houses, horses, donkeys. Try and see what you can do.

CUTTING OUT AND MAKING FLOWERS

For this you need brightly-coloured paper from which you will soon be able to cut out lovely flowers of all kinds. Below we give only a few examples of what can be done. You can make baskets of flowers or bouquets, just as you like.

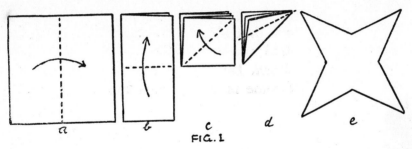

FIG. 1

Fig. 1. Fold a small square of paper as shown at *a*, *b*, *c*, and *d*. Now cut along the dotted line in *d*. Unfold, and you get a star like *e*. By folding several squares of paper at a time you can get lots of stars in one go.

FIG. 2

FIG. 3

FIG. 4

FIG. 5

FIG. 6

FIG. 7

Figs. 2 to *7.* Fold a small square of paper, as you did before for Fig. 1. Cut each time along the dotted line as shown in Figs. 2 to 7. Unfold and you get the different star, cross, or flowers shapes shown. Don't throw the cut-off bits of paper away. They may come in useful when you make a basket for your flowers.

FIG. 8

Fig. 8. Look carefully at this drawing and you will soon see how the various shapes can be pasted on top of each other to make pretty flowers. Give them stems and either make them into bouquets or put into baskets, like the one drawn. The basket is cut out from a folded piece of paper. See page 33, where the way to make leaves is also shown.

NET BAG

Fig. 1. Fold a square of thin paper as shown in Fig. 1 on page 41, *a*, *b*, and *c*.

Fig. 2. Cut slits in the folded paper, like this.

Fig. 3. Unfold completely. Take all four corners in one hand and shake your net out, like this.

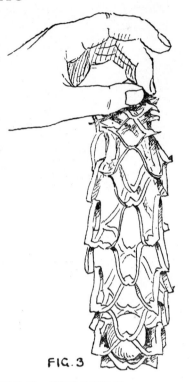

TABLE MAT—TABLE CENTRE

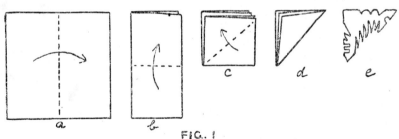

Fig. 1. Take a square piece of thin coloured paper and fold it in the way shown at *a*, *b*, and *c* above, so that it finally looks like *d*. Now trim the paper as at *e*.

FIG. 2

Fig. 2. Unfold what remains of your square, and this is how your table mat should look.

Fig. 3. Table Centre. Fold a square of thin coloured paper in the same way as in Fig. 1, *a*, *b*, and *c*. Fold *once again* as shown here at *p*, so that you get a shape like *q*. Now cut off the top along the dotted line. Trim what is left until you get a shape like *r*.

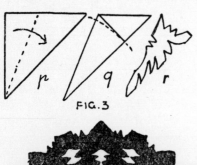

FIG. 3

FIG. 4

Fig. 4. Unfold the Table Centre. These mats and centres can, of course, be made in a variety of shapes.

44

ANOTHER NET BAG

Fig. 1. Fold and cut a square of thin paper as shown in Fig. 1 on page 43 (*a, b, c,* and *d*) and Fig. 3 (*p* and *q*). Cut slits up and down the remaining portion like this.

FIG. 1

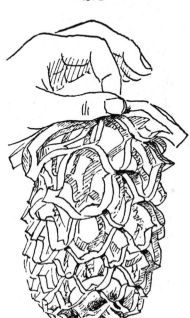

Fig. 2. Unfold, hold the ends, and shake out. There is your Net Bag!

FIG. 2

CHERRY PUZZLE

Fig. 1. Take an oblong piece of fairly stiff paper (a post card will do). On this draw and then cut two lines and a little circle. The round hole must be smaller than a cherry.

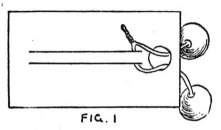

FIG. 1

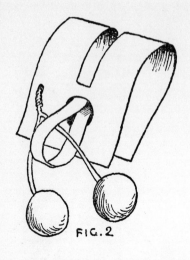

FIG. 2

Fig. 2. Bend the ends of the card nearly together, and pull the strip made by the two lines through the hole, so that you get a little loop, as shown here. Next, put one of your two cherries through the loop. You must, of course, have two cherries on one stalk.

Now get the loop and cherry stalks back into place, as in Fig. 1, and show it to your friends. Ask them if they can undo the cherries without damaging the card or the stalks. It will puzzle them, you can be sure of that.

Note. If you can't get cherries, try buttons or beads threaded on a piece of cotton or string.

46

TREES AND PLANTS

For these you need strong drawing paper, otherwise the trees will not stand up on their own. You will find these models very useful for adding to your farmyard (pages 37 and 40) or to the Churches, Buildings and Castles you will be making when you come to pages 66–77.

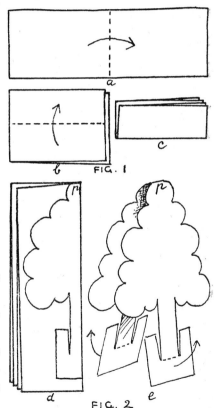

Fig. 1. Take a piece of paper (green paper is best) about three times as long as it is wide. Fold it as shown at *a*, *b*, and *c*.

Fig. 2. Draw and cut out the half-tree, as shown at *d*. You now have the two trees as in *e*, joined at the top *p*. Unfold the paper. Bend the bottom pieces in the direction of the arrows. The dotted line shows where your tree trunk ends.

FIG. 1

FIG. 2

47

FIG. 3

Fig. 3. Before fitting the flat bottom piece together like this, it is best to paste together the two straight pieces forming your tree trunk. The leafy part of the tree can be made to open out a little by pressing it down gently from the top.

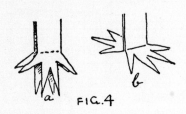

a   FIG. 4   b

Fig. 4. If you want to stick your tree to the ground, it is a good idea to trim the straight bottom portions first —as at *a*—then flatten out, like *b*, and paste down.

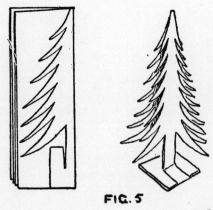

FIG. 5

Fig. 5. Draw and cut out this Fir Tree in exactly the same way. Dark green paper is best.

48

Fig. 6. This Palm Tree is also made in the same way. Cut snips in the leaves to make them look feathery.

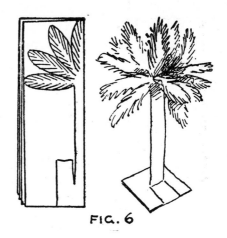

FIG. 6

Fig. 7. You will find it well worth while to take great care in cutting out this type of tree. When finished, twist the upper branches to make it look like a real tree.

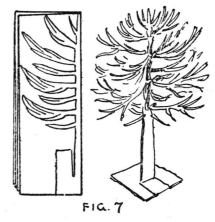

FIG. 7

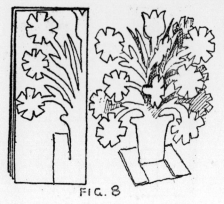

Fig. 8. Draw and make this vase of flowers in exactly the same way. Colour the flowers, just as you please.

FIG. 8

CATTLE PEN

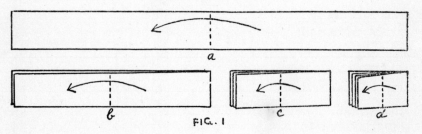

a

b   FIG. I   *c*   *d*

Fig. 1. Take a long strip of paper, measuring about 80 × 5 cm. Fold it, as shown in *a*, *b*, *c*, and *d*.

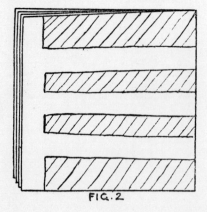

FIG. 2

Fig. 2. Cut out the shaded parts.

50

Fig. 3. Unfold your strip. You now have a long hedge or fence. Paste the ends together and curve this round into a Cattle or Sheep Pen, as shown. This sort of hedge will also come in useful for your farmyard, or for fencing off the Church and other buildings (pages 75–76).

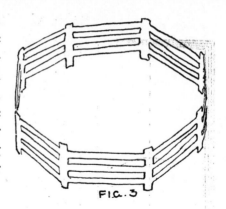

FIG. 3

DANCING FIGURES

Fig. 1. Fold a long strip of paper in the same way (Fig. 1 page 50). Draw and cut out this figure, taking care that the hands and feet come right to the edges of your paper at points *a*, *b*, *c*, and *d*.

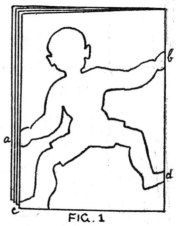

FIG. 1

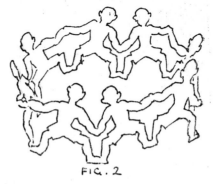

FIG. 2

Fig. 2. Unfold the strip. Paste the ends together. Now you have figures dancing Ring a Ring o' Roses.

51

ROYAL CROWN

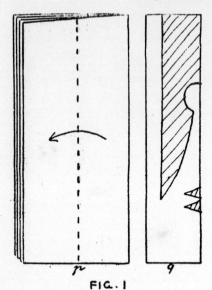

FIG. 1

Fig. 1. Take a long strip of paper, measuring about 50 × 14 cm. Fold it in the way shown in Fig. 1 on page 50. Now fold it once more, as shown at *p*. Cut away the three shaded parts shown in *q*.

FIG. 2

Fig. 2. Unfold your strip. It will look like this when you curve it into shape.

Fig. 3. Paste the ends of the strip together. Bring the tall straight pieces over to the centre, as shown, and stick them, where they overlap, on top of one another. Now your Crown should look like this—really royal!

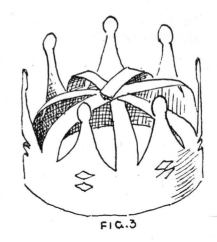

FIG.3

LACE BORDERS, FRIEZES

Fig. 1. Fold a strip of paper in the same way as before (Fig. 1, page 50). Fold it again as shown in Fig. 1 on page 52. Snip away the shaded parts, as in *a*.

Unfold your strip and you get Borders like these. Another way is to trim a folded strip in the manner shown at *b*.

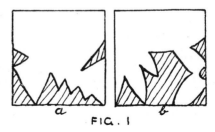

FIG. 1

FIG. 2

53

Fig. 2. Try your hand at other sorts. You can easily make fine Borders for lots of things. Ask Mother if she has a cupboard or kitchen shelf on which she would like a decorative Border pasted.

FANS

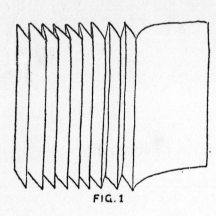

FIG. 1

Fig. 1. You need a long strip of medium-thick paper, measuring about 50 × 15 cm. Fold the paper like this, making each pleat about 3 cm. wide.

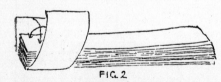

FIG. 2

Fig. 2. Round one end paste a strip of paper about 3 cm. wide, like this.

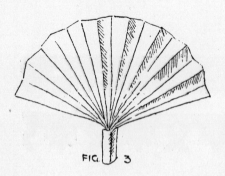

FIG. 3

Fig. 3. Spread out your Fan. What a nice surprise for Mother on a hot summer's day!

54

Fig. 4. This Fan is made in the same way, except that you need paper measuring about 20 × 75 cm. Round the block of folded pleats (see Fig. 2) paste a strip of paper about 12 cm. wide. When your handle is firmly fixed, pull out your Fan until it makes a complete circle. Paste the lower ends to the handle.

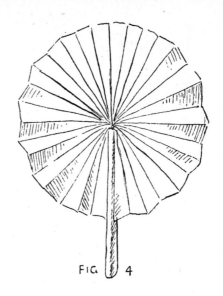

FIG. 4

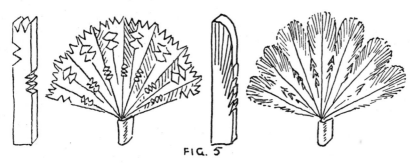

FIG. 5

Fig. 5. Here you see how you can improve your Fan-making.

MAGIC BOX

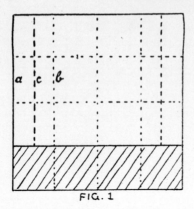

FIG. 1

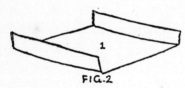

FIG. 2

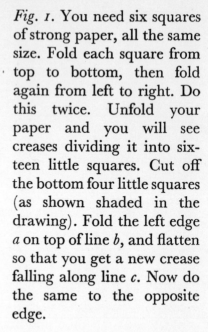

FIG. 3

Fig. 1. You need six squares of strong paper, all the same size. Fold each square from top to bottom, then fold again from left to right. Do this twice. Unfold your paper and you will see creases dividing it into sixteen little squares. Cut off the bottom four little squares (as shown shaded in the drawing). Fold the left edge *a* on top of line *b*, and flatten so that you get a new crease falling along line *c*. Now do the same to the opposite edge.

Fig. 2. Stand these folded edges upright, like this. Do the same with the other five squares of paper. Now lay your first piece flat on the table, as shown.

Fig. 3. Set your second and third pieces upright, like this, with their bottom edges underneath the first piece.

56

Fig. 4. Slide your fourth and fifth pieces into place, like this.

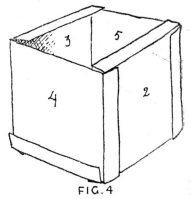

FIG.4

Fig. 5. Bring the sixth piece in its place, just like this, on top. Now you have a box which should not come apart. Try making boxes in different sizes. These shapes can, of course, be used as blocks or bricks for building houses.

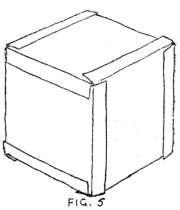

FIG. 5

Fig. 6. You can also make boxes to go inside one another. First construct a small box. Then *round it* make a bigger one. Before you start fastening up the bigger box, cut out little windows or stars, by folding each piece in two and cutting out the shaded bits, as shown.

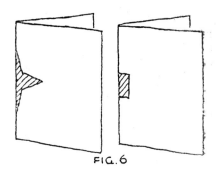

FIG.6

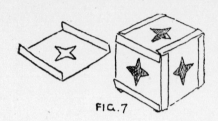

FIG.7

Fig. 7. The larger box will look like this. When people peep inside and see the smaller box, they will wonder how you managed to get it in.

TABLE

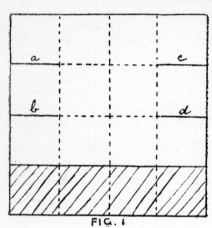

a   c

b   d

FIG. 1

Fig. 1. Take a square piece of strong paper, measuring about 16 × 16 cm. Make folds so that you have creases dividing the square into sixteen little squares (as you were shown in Fig. 1 on page 56). Now cut off the shaded portion and make slits along the lines *a*, *b*, *c*, and *d*.

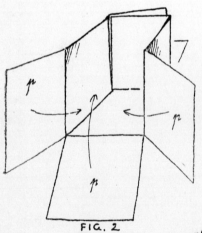

p

p

p

FIG. 2

Fig. 2. Bend the outer sides up like this, making an oblong box without a top. The three end squares *p* will overlap one another and must be pasted together, particularly along the edges and in the corners. Do the same with the three overlapping little squares at the other end.

58

Fig. 3. Turn your box upside down, like this. Now cut along the dotted lines. Do the same to the other sides of the box.

FIG. 3

Fig. 4. Paste a slightly bigger piece of paper on top, and there's your Table.

FIG. 4

CHAIR

Fig. 1. Fold a square piece of paper, measuring 12 × 12 cm., as shown in Fig. 1 on page 58. Cut the bottom shaded portion away, as before. Make slits along the lines *a, b, c,* and *d.* Now bend the portion between *a* and *b* (marked *back* in the drawing) upwards to form the back of the chair. Bend all the other squares downwards except the one marked *seat.*

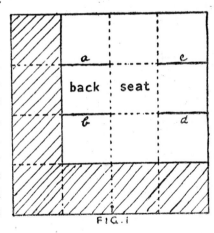

back seat

a   *c*

b   *d*

FIG. 1

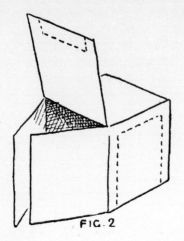

FIG. 2

Fig. 2. You get a shape like this. Paste the overlapping squares together, taking care that edges and corners are really well stuck. To make your chair-legs, cut along the dotted lines. Do the same to the other three sides. All that remains is to snip out a bit from the top of the back (see top dotted lines).

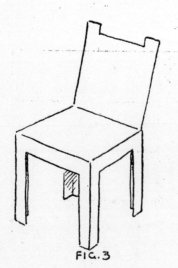

FIG. 3

Fig. 3. Your Chair should look like this.

DIVAN

Fig. 1. Take a square of strong paper 16 × 16 cm. and fold as for previous models (see Fig. 1 on page 58). Cut off the bottom squares so that your paper looks like this. Also slit the outer squares as before. Bend upwards a little strip, folding along the line AB.

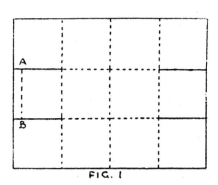

FIG. 1

Fig. 2. Now proceed just as if you were making the table on page 58. Keep the little square with the bent strip A to B up in the air, like this. Paste up all the rest and cut out the legs as before. Shorten the legs to the length you want.

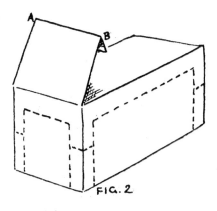

FIG. 2

Fig. 3. Bend over the part sticking up, like this. The strip A to B can now be pasted down on the divan, making a headrest or pillow.

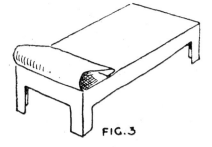

FIG. 3

61

BED

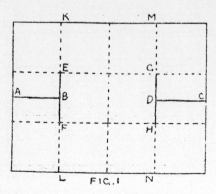

FIG. 1

Fig. 1. Take a square of strong paper, measuring 16 × 16 cm. Fold exactly as before (Fig. 1 on page 58). Cut off the bottom strip. Now cut slits along the lines A to B, E to F, and from C to D, G to H.

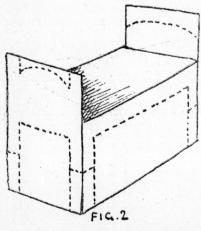

FIG. 2

Fig. 2. Bend down the top and lower strips of your paper along the lines EG and FH (Fig. 1 above). Fold the ends inwards so that they overlap, and you get a shape like this. Paste the overlapping ends. Now cut along the dotted lines. Shorten the legs just as you please.

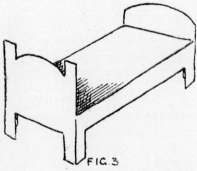

FIG. 3

Fig. 3. Here is the Bed finished. Another useful piece of furniture for the doll's house.

62

Fig. 1. Take a square of strong paper—one measuring 16 × 16 cm. would be a good size. Make creases in the paper by folding it from top to bottom, then from left to right. Do this *three times.* Unfold your square, and cut away the shaded portion. Make slits along the line A to B, and C to D.

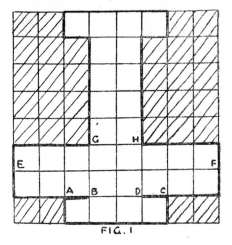

FIG. 1

Fig. 2. Lay your paper down like this. Brush a thin strip of paste just outside lines GB and HD (see shaded portions aside). Now bend both long side pieces towards the middle, as shown, so that edges E and F meet. You will now have bulges right and left, forming your two arm rests. Brush a strip of paste just above line GH where you see dots in the drawing. Bring the T-shaped portion over so that the top comes on line EF, and press down to stick on the paste. The unstuck portion will form a bulge. Your shape should look like Fig. 3. overleaf.

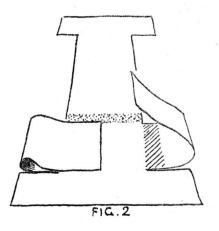

FIG. 2

63

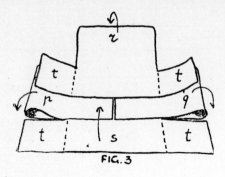

FIG. 3

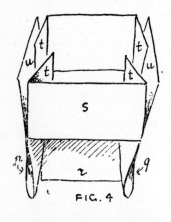

FIG. 4

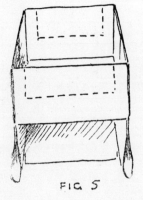

FIG 5

Fig. 3. Folding along line GH, bend downwards the part marked *r*. Both side pieces *t*, which are joined to *r*, will now come upright. Folding along lines BG and DH (see Fig. 1), bend the parts *p* and *q* downwards in the same way. Bend part *s* upwards, folding along line BD. Finally, bend all the four *t* pieces inwards. Your shape should now look like this.

Fig. 4. Paste all the parts marked *t* and stick them to sides *u*. Take particular care to see that all edges are well stuck together. Fig. 4 shows the armchair upside down; but, of course, not quite finished.

Fig. 5. Now for the legs. Cut along the dotted lines, as shown. Do the same at the sides.

64

Fig. 6. Turn the whole thing the right way up. There is your comfortable Armchair.

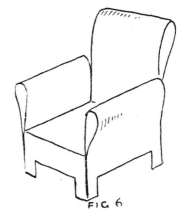

FIG 6

SETTEE

Fig. 1. This Settee is made in nearly the same way as the Armchair. The paper should be a quarter longer than it is wide—a piece 16 × 20 cm., for instance. First fold a 4-cm. strip back, so that you have a 16-cm. square. Now fold the square from top to bottom, and then from left to right. Do this three times (see Fig. 1 on page 63). Unfold the entire paper. You should now have nine creases running down and seven creases running across, dividing the paper into 80 little squares. Now, step by step, follow the instructions on pages 63 and 64 (Figs. 1 to 5).

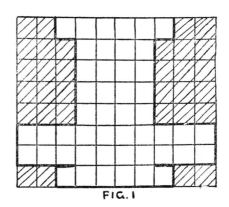

FIG. 1

E

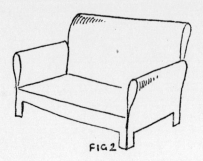

Fig. 2. This Settee, with two armchairs, will make a little suite for the sitting-room.

HOUSE AND GARAGE

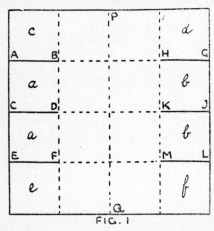

FIG. 1

Fig. 1. Take a square of strong paper, such as drawing paper. Fold the square from top to bottom, and from left to right. Do this twice. Unfold, and you should have creases where there are dotted lines in the drawing. Make slits from A to B, from C to D, and from E to F. On the opposite side make slits from G to H, J to K, and L to M. Now bend all the little squares *c*, *a*, *a*, *e*, and *d*, *b*, *b*, *f* upwards.

Fig. 2. Fold your paper in two, so that the two little squares *a* and the two little squares *b* overlap like this. Paste squares *a* together. Now stick squares *b* together. Your shape should look like this.

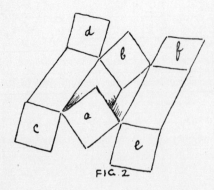

FIG. 2

66

Fig. 3. Fold the left side inwards until the squares *c* and *d* partly overlap *a* and *b* (as in the drawing). Paste *c* on *d* so that it remains stuck, exactly as in the drawing. Paste square *d* in the same way to the outside half of *b*. Now bend inwards the long right-hand strip. Squares *e* and *f* will partly overlap *c* and *d*. See that the top and bottom edges of squares *e* and *c* are in a straight line; then stick *e* on *c*. Do the same with *f* and *d*. Turn the whole thing upside down, and hey, presto!—a House.

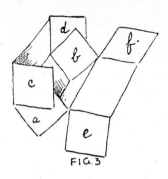

FIG.3

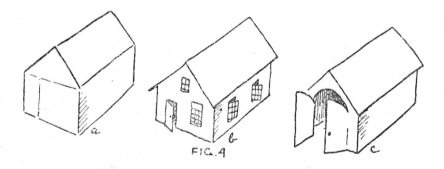

FIG.4

Fig. 4. Drawing *a* shows the plain building you have made. Paste another piece of paper on top of the house to make a roof. It should stick out a bit at the sides, as in *b*. Draw doors and windows. To make these so that they open, carefully cut along three of their four sides. To make a Garage, cut out big doors in front, as in *c*. In fact, there are all sorts of things you can do with this model.

SHED, PORCH, BUS-SHELTER

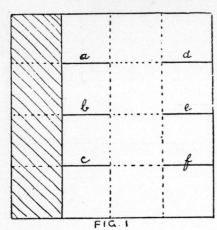

FIG. 1

Fig. 1. Take a square of strong paper and fold it as shown in Fig. 1 on page 66. Cut off the shaded part, and make slits along lines *a*, *b*, *c*, *d*, *e*, and *f*. Now go through all the steps and pastings given in Figs 2 and 3 on pages 66 and 67.

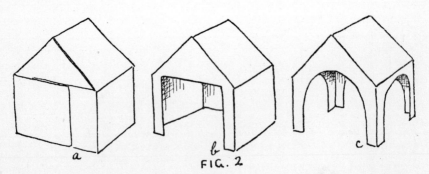

FIG. 2

Fig. 2. Here you have a smaller, but very useful, building. You can make all sorts of things from this. For instance, cut an open doorway as in *b*, and you get a Bus-shelter. By cutting out half-circles, as in *c*, you get a Porch.

68

CASTLE TOWER

Fig. 1. Fold a square of strong paper from top to bottom and from left to right *three times*, so that you get the same creases as there are dotted lines in the drawing. Cut out the shaded part, but do not throw it away. You can now start to make two Towers from the two parts left. Make slits in one part along the lines *a*, *b*, *c*, and *d*.

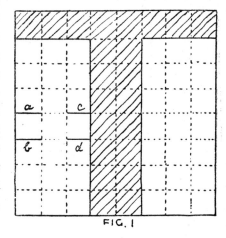

FIG. 1

Fig. 2. Fold your paper like this. Now make *f* stand upright, and paste it, at the top, on *e*. Do the same to the other side. Next, bring *g* inwards and paste it on *f*. Do the same to the other side.

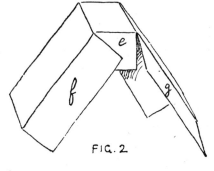

FIG. 2

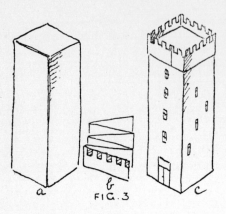

FIG. 3

Fig. 3. The shape is now like *a*. Take a strip of four squares from the shaded part you cut out in Fig. 1. Fold the strip as in *b*. Cut out the little shaded parts. Now paste this strip of embattlements round the top of the tower, as in *c*. Draw doors and windows. There stands your proud Castle Tower.

CLOCK TOWER, CHURCH TOWER, WINDMILL, ETC.

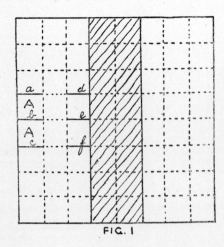

FIG. 1

Fig. 1. Take a square of strong paper and fold it three times as before (Fig. 1 on page 66). Cut out the shaded portion. This will leave portions for two Towers or Windmills. Make slits along lines *a*, *b*, *c*, and *d*, *e*, *f*. Tuck one A square behind the other and paste together. Do the same with the two opposite little squares.

70

Fig. 2. Fold your paper to this shape. Bend portion B inwards and paste it at the top to A. Bend portion C inwards and paste it to B. Do the same with the pieces at the back.

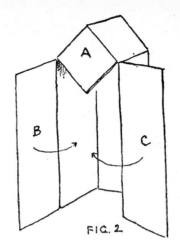

FIG. 2.

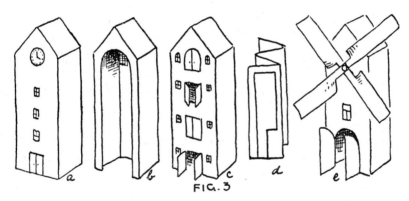

FIG. 3.

Fig. 3. To turn this into a Clock Tower draw a clock, as in *a*. Add, if you wish, windows and doors. For a Sentry Box cut out the portion in front, as shown in *b*. The drawing *c* shows the old-fashioned warehouse often seen along Dutch canals. Doors and windows are drawn and cut out as shown. For a Windmill, fold another piece of paper in pleats, as in *d*, and cut out four sails in one go. Paste the four sails on the Windmill, as in *e*. Pencil in a window or two, cut out double doors —and there is a Windmill just as in Holland.

SHACK, BARN, BEACH HUT, ARCHES

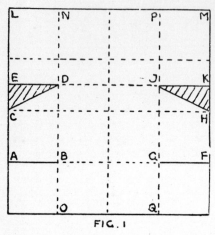

FIG. 1

Fig. 1. Fold a square of strong paper from top to bottom and from left to right *twice*, so that you get creases giving you 16 little squares. Fold top edge LM down on line AF. Flatten, unfold, and you get a new crease-line, EK. Make slits along lines ED, AB, KJ, and FG. Now cut sloping slits from C to D; and from H to J. Remove the shaded portions. The portion between DJ and BG will be the top of your Shack. Fold all the other parts downwards.

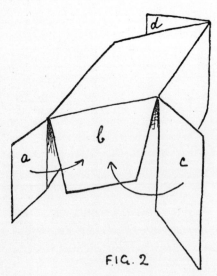

FIG. 2

Fig. 2. Hold it so that it looks like this. Paste *a* on *b*, and *c* on *b*. Do the same at the other end. Cut away unwanted *d* bits.

72

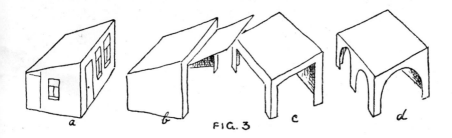

Fig. 3. By drawing doors and windows, as in *a* above, you get a little Shack or Bungalow. Snip out the front, as in *b*, and you have a Shed with a canopy in front; this could also be a Beach Hut. The drawing *c* shows how you can cut out even more, and make other types of Shelters, Sheds, or Out-houses. By cutting out half-circles, as in *d*, archways or arcades can be made.

BRIDGE

Fig. 1. Fold a square of strong paper as in Fig. 1 on page 72. Cut away the shaded part. Make four slits as marked by *a*, and four tiny slits, as at *b*.

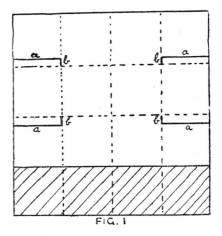

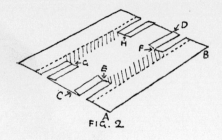

FIG. 2

Fig. 2. Fold back the small strips made by these slits, like this. Fold edge AB over so that it falls along CD. Press, unfold, and you get a new crease where the dotted line is shown in the drawing. Fold the opposite edge over so that it falls on line GH and so get another crease. Brush a little paste in the two shaded positions inside the two new creases. Bend edge AB and the opposite edge inwards again on to lines EF and GH, so that they are held down by the paste. Now bend the sides of the bridge downwards, so that they both stand upright.

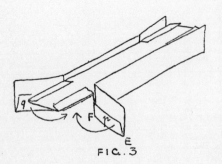

FIG. 3

Fig. 3. The shape should look like this. Cut along line EF so that portion *p* can be swung inwards. Do the same with portion *q*, and then paste it to portion *p*. By doing likewise at the other end of the bridge you get supporting pieces underneath.

Fig. 4. Paste little strip *r* on to *s* like this. Do the same with the other three little strips. Now snip along the side of your bridge as shown by dotted lines in the drawing. Do the same on the other side.

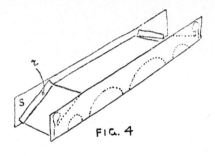

FIG. 4

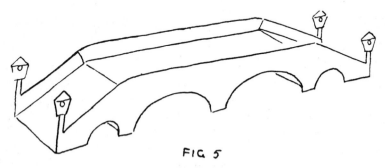

FIG 5

Fig. 5. Draw lights on your lamp-standards—and now you have this fine bridge.

CHURCH

This Church is one of the many things that can be made by putting together some of the models made when working through pages 66 to 72. The little tower half-way along the church roof is made in exactly the same way as the shed or little house shown in *a* of Fig.

75

2 on page 68. You only have to snip out a small portion front and back so that it fits neatly on both sides of the roof.

See pages 47 to 49 for the way to make trees.

FACTORY

For all the parts shown here, go back to the things we made on pages 66 to 72. The chimney-stack is made from a rolled-up piece of paper.

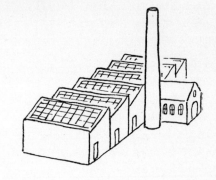

CASTLE

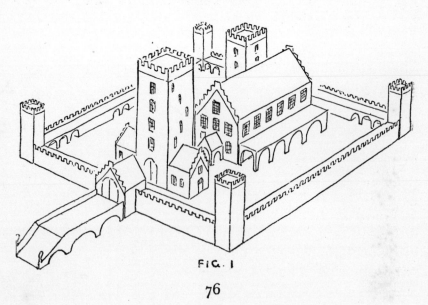

FIG. 1

Fig. 1. Just look closely at this Castle. It is made by putting together the various models described on pages 66 to 75. The only new things are the Walls and the ornamental ends of the roofs (called Gables). The way to make these is given in Figs. 2 and 3 below.

Some of the other things will need to be altered a little to make them fit. The Bridge, for instance (Fig. 5 on page 75), will have to have one of its ends cut off. The covered column (or Colonnade) on the right of the Castle is made by cutting out half-circles for Archways in the oblong box you were shown the way to make in Fig. 3 on page 59.

You can be even cleverer and build up, in the same way, a *whole* village or town—with all sorts of houses, farms, windmills, etc., gathered round a Town Hall or Church.

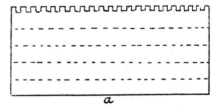

Fig. 2. Castle Walls. Take a piece of strong paper. Cut it at the top, as shown in *a*. Fold along the dotted lines, as in *b*. Paste the two inner sides together, as in *c*. Archways and doors can now be cut out, just as you like.

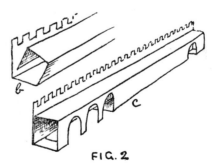

FIG. 2

Fig. 3. Gables. To make ornamental ends for your roofs, fold a square piece of paper as shown in *a* and *b*. Snip little notches in two edges, as in *c*. Cut off the shaded part. Now you have four gable-ends. Don't make them too small. After fixing, you can always trim off any overhanging pieces.

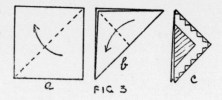

FIG 3

SLEIGH, SLEDGE

FOLD

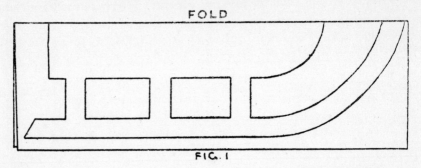

FIG. 1

Fig. 1. Take a piece of strong paper and fold it in two, so that the crease comes at the top. Draw lines and curves as shown above. Cut along your lines, and then unfold your paper.

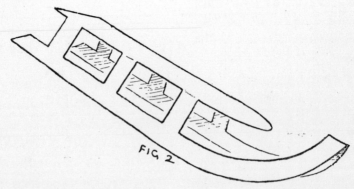

FIG 2

Fig. 2. Flatten, and smooth out the crease. Bend the sides straight down, as shown above. A real Dutch sledge!

78

FOLDING TABLE, CARD TABLE, STOOL

Fig. 1. Take an oblong piece of strong paper, such as drawing paper or cardboard, twice as long as it is wide. Fold it in two so that the crease is at the top. Now cut away the shaded portions. Take care not to make the legs too short.

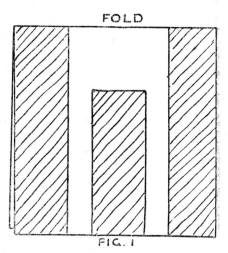

FOLD

FIG. 1

Fig. 2. Unfold your paper and smooth the middle portion flat. Half-way along each leg make a slit up, or down, as shown. The slit should be half the width of the leg. Bend the legs downwards.

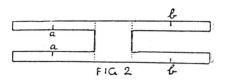

FIG. 2

Fig. 3. Push each pair of legs together so that the slits link (see also Fig. 5 on page 21). Here is your Folding Stool or Card Table.

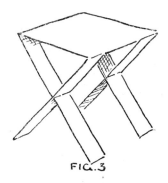

FIG. 3

79

GARDEN TABLE

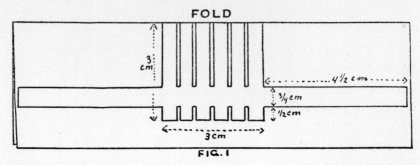

FOLD

3 cm

4½ cm

¾ cm

½ cm

3 cm

FIG. 1

Fig. 1. Take a piece of strong paper, such as drawing paper or cardboard, measuring about 12 × 12 cm. Fold it in two so that the crease comes at the top. Carefully draw lines to the exact measurements shown above; and then cut along the lines.

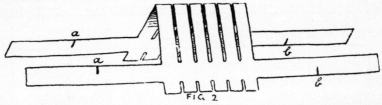

a

a

b

b

FIG. 2

Fig. 2. Unfold your paper. Smooth the middle portion flat. Cut slits in the legs, as shown *down* at *a* and *up* at *b*. These slits should be just half the width of each leg.

Fig. 3. Bend your legs downwards and link the slits in each pair. There stands your Garden Table.

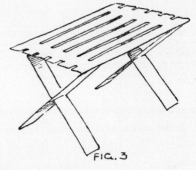

FIG. 3

GARDEN CHAIR

FOLD

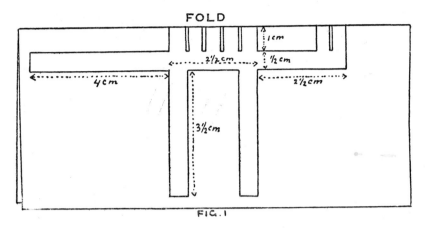

FIG. I

Fig. 1. Take a square of strong paper such as drawing paper or cardboard, measuring 12 × 12 cm. Fold it in two with the crease at the top. Draw lines carefully to the exact measurements shown. Then cut along these lines.

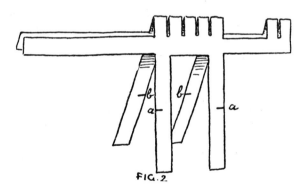

FIG. 2

Fig. 2. Unfold your paper and smooth out the middle crease. Make slits as at *a* and *b* above in each pair of legs. The slits should be half the width of the legs.

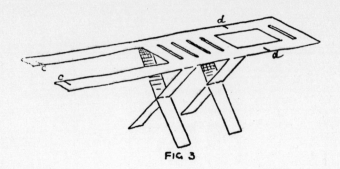

FIG 3

Fig. 3. Bend the legs down, and link the slits in each pair. Now make fresh slits, half-way across each strip, at the four places marked *c* and *d* above. The *d* slits should be just half-way along the *open* back of your chair.

Fig. 4. Straighten up the back of your chair. Bend the two arm-rests up and back, as shown. Fit the rests into the back of the chair by linking the two pairs of slits. A pair of these chairs, with the table you have made (see page 80,) would be very useful in a garden.

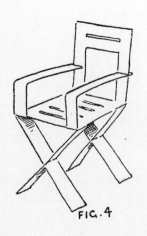

FIG. 4

WHEELBARROW

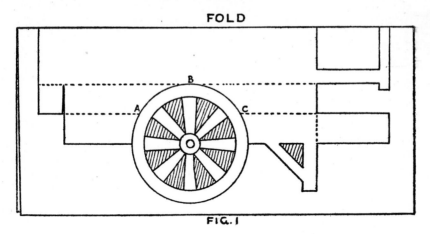

FIG. 1

Fig. 1. Take a 12 × 12 cm. square of strong paper such as drawing paper and fold it in two so that the crease is at the top. With your ruler and compass draw the above design. Cut along the plain *straight* lines. *Don't* cut along the dotted lines. Now cut along the *bottom* half of the wheel. With a sharp penknife cut out the shaded portions in the wheel. Next cut along the curved portion from A to B, and from B to C, so that most—*but not all*—your wheel is cut.

Fig. 2. Unfold your paper and smooth out the middle crease. Brush paste on the shaded portions. Bend the two outer sides, including the wheels, inwards (folding along the dotted line) and press flat until they are well stuck.

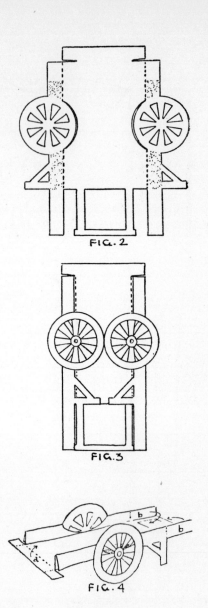

FIG. 2

Fig. 3. Your Wheelbarrow should now look like this. Folding along the dotted lines, bend the wheel side pieces downwards at both sides. Turn the Wheelbarrow round and make sure it now looks like the one in Fig. 4.

FIG. 3

Fig. 4. Brush a little paste on the ends of strip *a*. Then bend *a* upwards along the dotted line. Tuck the ends between the double sides of the Wheelbarrow. Press until the paste holds. At the other end, fold the pieces *b* inwards (see arrows) and paste the ends together.

FIG. 4

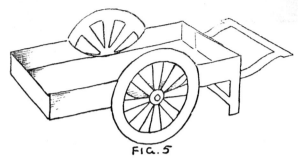

FIG. 5

Fig. 5. Although the wheels cannot be made to turn, the barrow itself looks just the job, doesn't it?

RED INDIAN FEATHERS, FUNNY MASKS

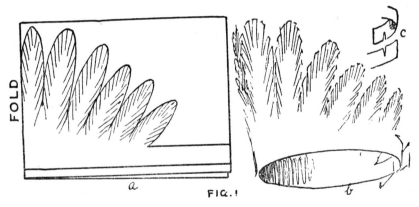

FOLD

a

FIG. 1

b

c

Fig. 1. Take a piece of strong paper, such as drawing paper, measuring about 25 × 70 cm. Fold it in two, so that the crease is on the left. Draw the design in *a* above, and then cut it out. Cut tiny snips into the feathers, as you did for Fig. 4 on page 27. Unfold your paper.

In one band cut a slit half-way *up*, and in the other band a slit half-way *down*, as in *c*. Link the bands together, as in *b*. Now put it on—and you are a Red Indian Chief. *How!*

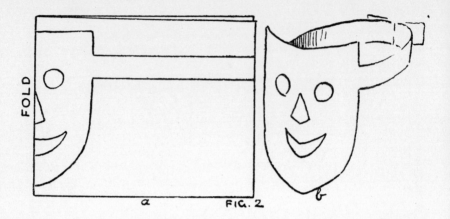

Fig. 2. For this sort of Mask you need a long piece of paper. Fold it in two with the crease on the left. Draw and cut out the design in *a*. Unfold your paper. Try the mask for size. Where the bands overlap at the back of your head, cut slits to link them, as before.

Fig. 3. Make this mask in the same way, but do not cut out a space for your nose—just cut along the plain lines given in *a*.

Cut lots of slits for hair and beard. Ruffle them a bit to make them look real, as in *b*.

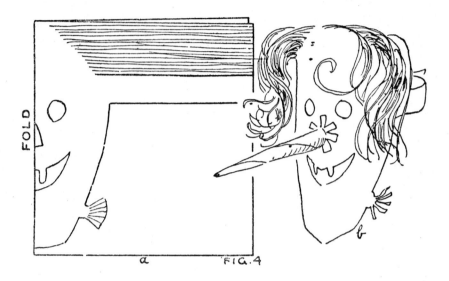

a   FIG. 4

Fig. 4. This weird affair is made on the same lines. When it is cut out, snip one of the warts off the face, and part the hair down each side, ruffling it wildly as in *b*. Make the funny nose by rolling up another piece of paper crossways and pasting the loose end so that it doesn't unroll. Cut small slits in the broad end and bend outwards the slitted portions. Stick the nose on the face, as in *b*. Come into the room with this on at Christmas, and everybody will shriek with laughter.

AEROPLANE

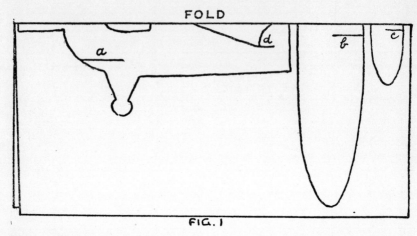

FIG. 1

Fig. 1. Fold a square of strong paper (drawing paper) or cardboard in two, with the crease at the top. Draw and cut out the Aeroplane body, wing, and tail, as given above. Cut slits at *a*, *b*, *c*, and *d*.

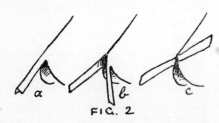

FIG. 2

Fig. 2. Cut the strip in front of the Aeroplane body in two. Bend the two cut portions (see *b*) to make the propeller, as *c*.

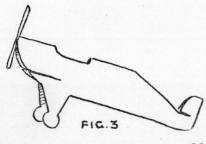

FIG. 3

Fig. 3. Open out and stand the body up like this.

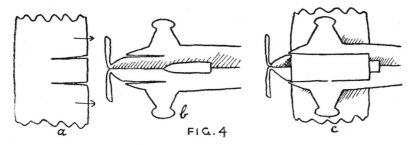

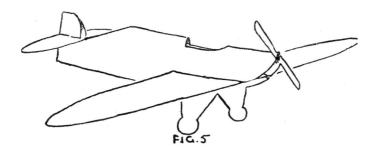

FIG. 4

Fig. 4. Unfold the big wings and push them into place, linking their slits with those at *a* on the front of the plane. Drawing *c* shows (from underneath) the middle part of the wings fitted well into the aeroplane body.

FIG. 5

Fig. 5. Unfold the smaller wings, smooth out flat, and insert into the tailpiece, linking the slits in both. Now you have the complete Aeroplane.

FOUR-ENGINED PASSENGER PLANE

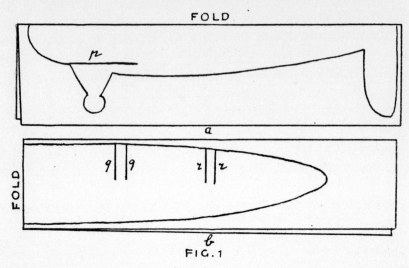

FIG.1

Fig. 1. Several pieces of strong paper are required. To make the plane-body, fold one piece with the crease at the top as in *a*. For the big wings fold another piece with the crease on the left, as in *b*. Draw the above outlines, and cut out as before. Make slits at *p*, *q*, and *r*. Unfold and smooth out the wings.

Fig. 2. Fold a smaller piece of paper with the crease at the top. Draw the design and cut out, making slit as shown. This is one of the four engines you will need to make.

Fig. 3. Unfold the engine slightly and fit, by its slits, into the double wing slits (*q* or *r* of Fig. 1).

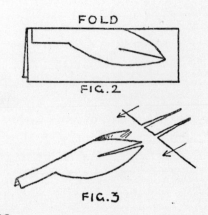

Fig. 4. Cut the strip in front of the engine into four narrower strips, like this.

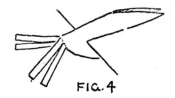

FIG. 4

Fig. 5. Bend the four narrow strips to form a propeller, like this.

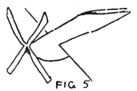

FIG 5

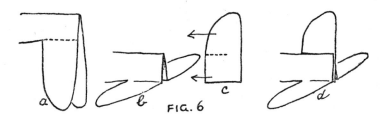

a   b   FIG. 6   c   d

Fig. 6. Now to finish off the plane tail. Bend the side pieces upwards on the dotted line as in *a* above, so that they both spread out flat, as in *b*. Make a small slit along the top right-hand fold of *b*. From a smaller piece of paper cut out a rudder, shaped like *c*. Cut a slit in this (see dotted line). Push the rudder in the direction of the arrows on the tail, so that slits link together. Rudder and tail should now look like *d*.

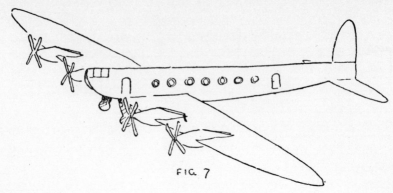

FIG. 7

Fig. 7. Make three more engines and place them on the big wings as above. Now fit the wings into the plane as you did before (Fig. 4 on page 89). Draw windows and doors on the plane body—and your overseas passenger aeroplane is made.

You can make different sorts of aeroplanes in the same way. What is more, by using models such as you have made already (pages 66 to 76), you can construct an entire airport.

A STEAMSHIP

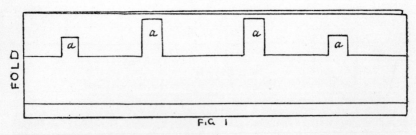

FOLD

FIG. 1

Fig. 1. Fold a long strip of strong paper in two, so that the crease is on the left, as above. Cut out the model as shown. The portions labelled *a* can be placed just as you like. Those in the middle should be a little bigger than those towards the ends of the ship.

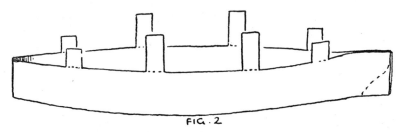

FIG . 2

Fig. 2. Paste the two (rudder) ends of the ship together and cut along the dotted line to form a stern. Bend the upright strips (*a* of Fig. 1) towards the middle.

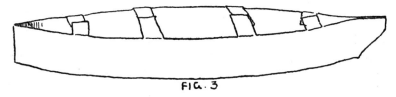

FIG. 3

Fig. 3. Make these strips overlap one another to the shape and width *you* would like your ship, and paste them together.

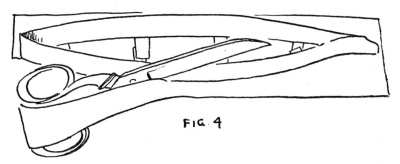

FIG. 4

Fig. 4. Now apply more paste on top of the strips you have just stuck together. Turn the ship upside down and lay it on a flat piece of strong paper. Press the strips down so that they stick to the flat piece of paper. Then cut the flat piece, as above, to the shape of your ship. This will be your deck. Do not let the stern end in too sharp a point.

93

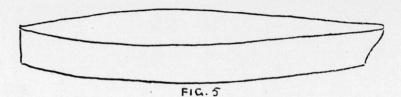

FIG. 5

Fig. 5. This is how the hull of the ship should look.

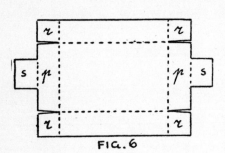

FIG. 6

Fig. 6. To complete the ship you need a strong piece of paper. Cut it out like this, with slits at *r*. Fold back the top and bottom strips along the dotted lines.

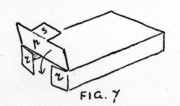

FIG. 7

Fig. 7. Bend portion *p* like this, and paste it on the squares *r*. Do the same at the other end. Apply paste underneath *s* and now stick entire piece on your deck (see Fig. 9).

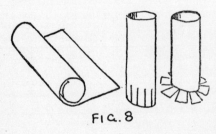

FIG. 8

Fig. 8. Make a funnel by rolling up a piece of paper and pasting one end, so that it cannot unroll. In the bottom end cut slits. Flatten out the pieces you've made, like this. Paste them on the deck.

94

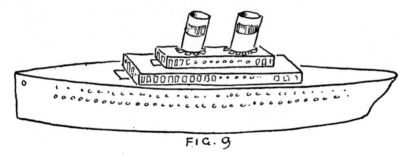

FIG. 9

Fig. 9. Here is a big passenger ship with two decks and two funnels. You can, if you like, add masts (see Fig. 4 on page 96) for aerial, loading, etc., purposes.

A SAILING YACHT

FOLD

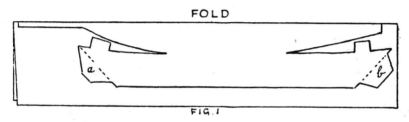

FIG. 1

Fig. 1. Fold a piece of strong paper in two with the crease at the top. Draw and cut out the deck and hull, as shown above. The upper part which will be your deck (see also Fig. 3 on page 96) should be narrower than the lower part or hull. Fig. 1 shows a very small model. The Yacht you make can of course be much larger. Fold the end pieces *a* and *b* (along the dotted lines) towards the inside.

CENTRE FOLD

deck

hull

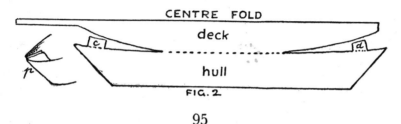

FIG. 2

95

Fig. 2. Paste *a* and *b* together, as at *p* overleaf. Fold the little pieces *c* and *d* inwards along the dotted lines. Unfold your deck and smooth out the crease. Folding on the dotted lines, bend your hull downwards.

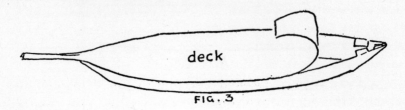

deck

FIG. 3

Fig. 3. Stick down the deck fore and aft on the four pieces *c* and *d*. Your hull is now complete. You may, of course, have to trim your deck round, so that it fits neatly.

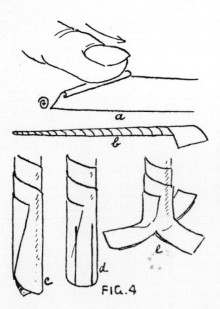

FIG. 4

Fig. 4. To make a mast you need a long narrow strip of strong paper. Roll this up in the way shown in *a* and *b*. When it is long enough, paste the end so that it does not unroll. Trim the thick end *c* straight, as at *d*. Make a few slits from the bottom of the mast, bend these portions outwards, and paste them to the deck of your yacht so that your mast stands upright in the position shown in Fig. 5.

96

Fig. 5. Lay the hull with its mast on top of a piece of thin, but strong, paper, like this. Now you will be able to judge the size of your foresail. In the drawing the sail is shown by the dotted lines. Draw these lines on the flat thin paper.

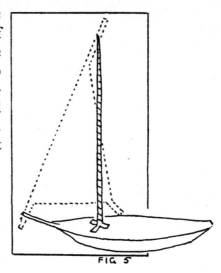

FIG 5

Fig. 6. Cut along the lines you have drawn. Hold your foresail as shown, and with the right thumb and first finger, gently smooth a curve into it. Follow the direction of the arrow. Be careful that the sail does not tear.

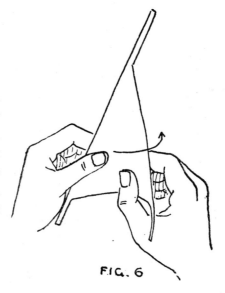

FIG. 6

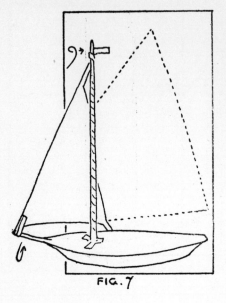

FIG. 7

Fig. 7. Get the sail into place by smearing the hanging strip on the left with paste and linking it round the bowsprit, as shown, and then up on to the sail itself. Press it so that it sticks to both the bowsprit and the sail. In the same way, paste and twist the top strip of the sail round the top of the mast. You can leave a loose bit of the strip to serve as a flag. Next, paste the other bottom right-hand strip to the side of the yacht.

Lay the yacht down again on another flat piece of thin, strong paper to get an idea of the required size, and darw lines like the dotted ones.

Fig. 8. Add portions *p* and *q* to your drawing and then cut out the whole of the larger figure.

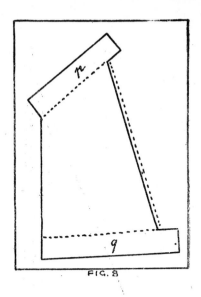

FIG. 8

Fig. 9. Roll portion *p* downwards, as tightly as you can (see arrows for direction), and paste down. In the same way, tightly roll up and stick the portion *q* to the bottom of the sail, just as in the drawing. Sailors call these pieces 'gaff' and 'gig'. They steady the sail. With thumb and forefinger make a curve in the sail (as you did for Fig. 6 on page 97).

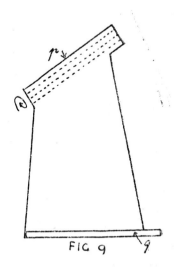

FIG 9

99

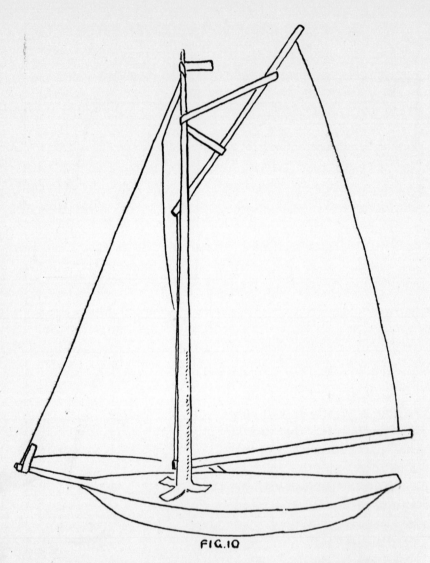

FIG.10

Fig. 10. Paste the left-hand side of your mainsail to the mast. For support, twist and paste a thin strip of paper round the mast, near the top. Stick the ends of the strip on the gaff, as shown above. Now you have your Yacht.

A THREE-MASTER SAILING SHIP

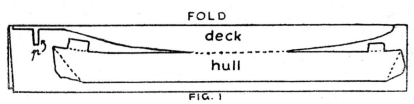

FOLD

deck

hull

FIG. 1

Fig. 1. Fold a piece of strong paper (drawing paper or cardboard) in two, with the crease at the top. Draw the deck and the hull, as shown. Cut out and make your ship, with its masts, just as you made the sailing Yacht (Figs. 1–4, pages 95–96). At the left, paste parts *p* together.

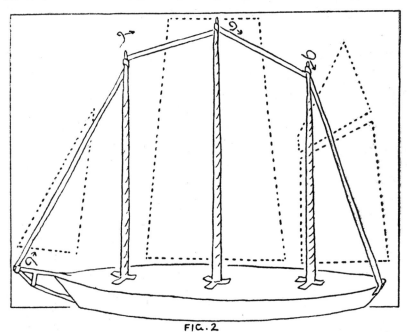

FIG. 2

Fig. 2. Take a long, very narrow strip of strong paper. Stick one end to the front side of the ship. Paste the strip again where it reaches the lower end of *p*. Now twist it round, and stick it to the tip of the bowsprit (see arrow). Next, carry the strip up to the top of the first mast. After brushing a little paste on the strip, twist it round the mast. Then go on and do the same round the second and third masts. When you come to the stern, paste the end of the strip firmly on the side.

Lay your ship, with its masts, down gently on a big sheet of strong thin paper. Look at the dotted lines. Make drawings like these on your big sheet. Then cut these sails out.

Fig. 3. Copy these drawings on your big middle sail, and cut out along the plain lines, thus making four small sails for your middle mast as shown in Fig. 6. Fold (along the dotted line) and paste down the upper portion of each small sail, so that you get a steadying yard-arm above it.

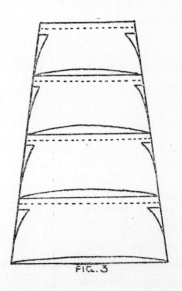

FIG. 3

Fig. 4. With thumb and forefinger curve each sail as in Fig. 6, page 97. Apply paste to the yard-arm and centre of each sail (where shaded), then stick the sails against the middle mast (see Fig. 6). For the front mast, cut out four slightly smaller sails, and again follow the methods given in Figs. 2, 3, and 4.

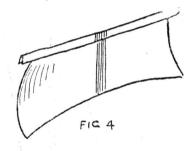

FIG 4

Fig. 5. Other sails on the fully-rigged ship are made in the same way as the sails of the Yacht (pages 98 and 99). Fasten the *fore* sails by their three strips on the hull and the mast. Make three or four such sails and place several in front of the ship. Put one also before the third mast to balance it. Make the top *aft*sail as shown aside on the same pattern as Figs. 8–9 page 99.

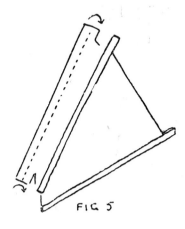

FIG 5

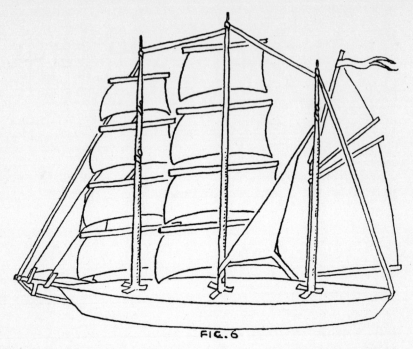

FIG. 6

Fig. 6. Attach flags or pennants to your masts or topsails as you like. Now you have your Three-master Sailing Ship, a real work of art. Other types of ships are given below.

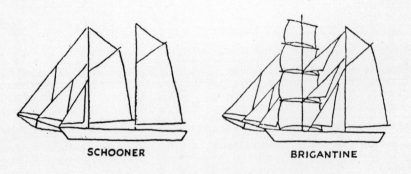

SCHOONER   BRIGANTINE

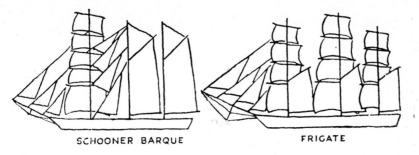

SCHOONER BARQUE   FRIGATE

Fig. 7. These are different sorts of sailing ships. All can be tackled on the lines already shown.

FUNNY CLOWN

Fig. 1. This is an easily-made comic figure, and you can use any paper provided it is not too thin. Draw and cut out a clown's body and head as shown here (or you can make a funny shape to your own fancy). Cut out four slits at positions *a*, for the arms and legs to go through.

FIG. 1

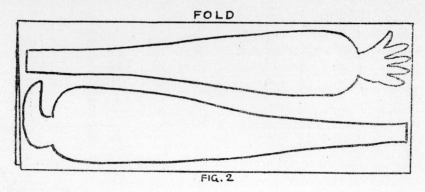

FIG. 2

Fig. 2. Fold a piece of paper in two so that the crease is at the top. Cut out the arms and legs, as shown.

Fig. 3. Push the arms and legs through the slits in the body. At the back of the body paste the plain ends of the arms firmly together. Paste the ends of the legs in the same way. Now paste both pairs together, as shown.

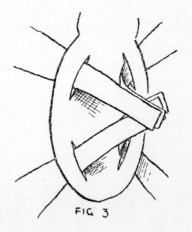

FIG 3

Fig. 4. Hold the body with one hand. With the other hand waggle the arms and legs about by pushing these joined ends in and out a bit. You will soon succeed in making the clown cut all sorts of funny capers.

FIG. 4

ROCKING HORSE

FOLD

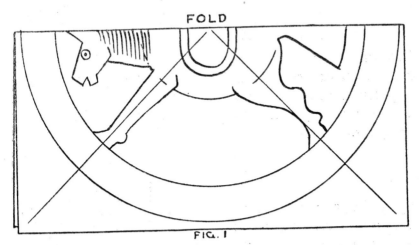

FIG. I

Fig. 1. Fold a square of strong paper, such as drawing paper or cardboard, in two, with the crease at the top. With a com-

107

pass draw three half-circles, as overleaf. The top semi-circle is
drawn simply to help you draw the horse. Look at Fig. 2 and
cut carefully along the lines, so that you get the shape you
see below.

Fig. 2. Cut off the top portions of the semicircles above
line O. In the *top* layer only
of the semicircle cut slits
running half-way across at
p. Folding on dotted line
r, tuck backwards the *top*
layers left and right. Turn
your shape around.

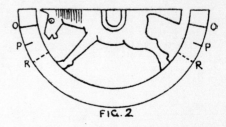

FIG. 2

Fig. 3. Now it looks like this.
Cut half-way slits, as at *s*, in
the other layer of the semi-
circle left and right. Folding
on dotted line T, bend these
portions backwards too.

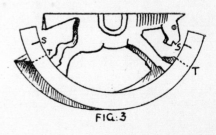

FIG. 3

Fig. 4. The folded two pairs
of ends can now be linked
together by their slits, like
this.

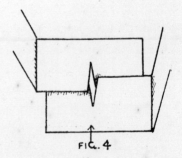

FIG. 4

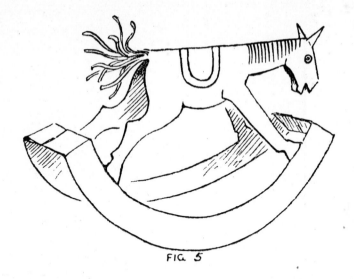

FIG. 5

Fig. 5. Slit the tail into thin strips, as shown. Cut the ears apart and bend them more upright. Quite a good Rocking Horse, isn't it?

DACHSHUND OR SAUSAGE DOG

FOLD

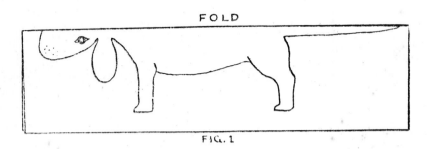

FIG. 1

Fig. 1. Take a piece of strong paper and fold it in two with the crease at the top. Draw and cut out the Dachshund, as above.

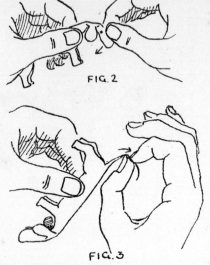

FIG. 2

Fig. 2. Hold the shape firmly, like this, and bend the head downwards (see arrow). This will make the ears stand out.

FIG. 3

Fig. 3. Let the tail slide through the thumb and fore-finger, like this. The tail will then curl upwards.

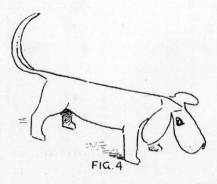

FIG. 4

Fig. 4. Here is your Dachs-hund or Sausage Dog. Now give him a present—a collar and a name.

SWAN

Fig. 1. Fold a piece of strong paper in two, so that the crease comes at the bottom. Draw and cut out a swan, like this, and cut slits for the feathers. Now take the upper layer of your folded paper, and, folding along the dotted line, bend it towards you, and downwards, so that the swan above the dotted line is bent right over the lower part. Turn your shape round and fold the other layer in the same way.

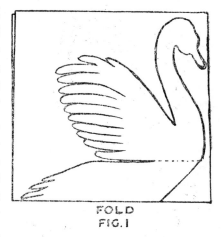

FOLD
FIG. 1

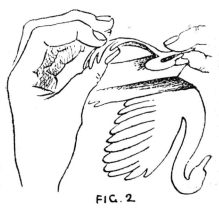

Fig. 2. Curve the wings like this, letting them glide through your fingers.

FIG. 2

111

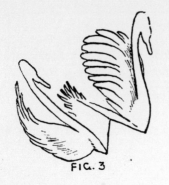

FIG. 3

Fig. 3. The shapes now should look like this. Brush paste on the inside of the heads and necks, and press them together.

FIG. 4

Fig. 4. Make the tail feathers stick up a little. Here is the Swan ready to take to the water.

DUCKS AND DUCKLINGS

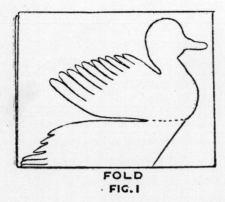

FOLD
FIG. 1

Fig. 1. Fold a piece of strong paper so that the crease comes at the bottom. Draw this design. Cut out and make your Duck in the same way as you did your swan (page 111).

Fig. 2. From another piece, folded with the crease at the bottom, cut three Ducklings like this, and proceed as before.

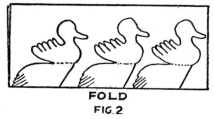

FOLD
FIG. 2

Fig. 3. Place your Duck and Ducklings like this, in one happy family.

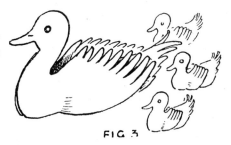

FIG 3

ELEPHANT

FOLD

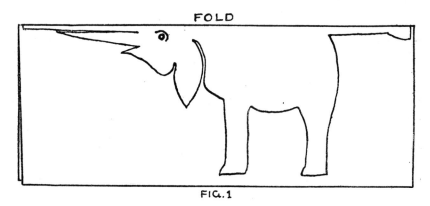

FIG. 1

Fig. 1. The Elephant is made from strong paper, folded in two, with the crease at the top. Draw the design and cut out.

H 113

Fig. 2. Cut slits in the end of the tail to make it look more like a tassel. Bend both head and tail downwards.

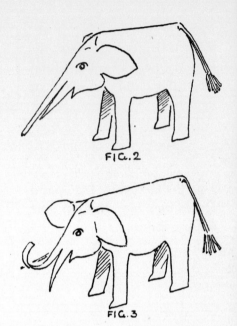

FIG. 2

Fig. 3. With your thumb and forefinger (as in Fig. 3 on page 110), make the trunk curl upwards. Bend the ears outwards and separate the tusks a little. Now your Elephant is ready to go to the Zoo.

FIG. 3

GRAZING COW

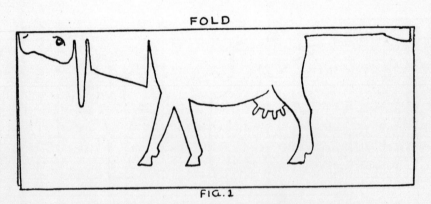

FOLD

FIG. 1

Fig. 1. Fold a peice of strong paper so that the crease comes on top. Draw and cut out the cow, as above.

Fig. 2. Make a sort of tassel at the end of the tail by cutting small slits in it. Bend both head and tail downwards. Curl the horns upwards.

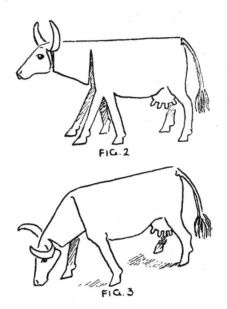

Fig. 3. You still have four front legs on your cow. That won't do, will it? From the top layer of your paper cut off the leg in front. From the other layer cut off the rear leg. Now, by pressing the neck of the cow downwards, you can make it stand, grazing contentedly like this.

CHRISTMAS ANGEL

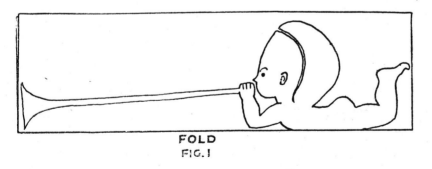

FOLD
FIG. 1

Fig. 1. Fold a piece of strong paper in two, so that the crease comes at the bottom. Draw and cut out the above design.

115

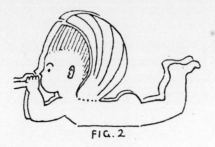

Fig. 2. Draw these lines on the head and wings; then cut out slits along the lines.

FIG. 2

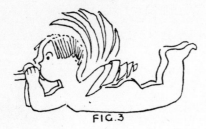

Fig. 3. Bend hair and wings outwards on both layers of paper.

FIG. 3

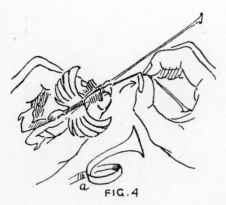

Fig. 4. Hold your shape like this, and, by letting each trumpet in turn glide between the nails of your thumb and forefinger, form curls in both trumpets, as shown at *a*.

FIG. 4

FIG. 5

Fig. 5. Paste the halves forming the head and body together. Open the arms and legs a little; and lo and behold—a Christmas Angel!

PEACOCK

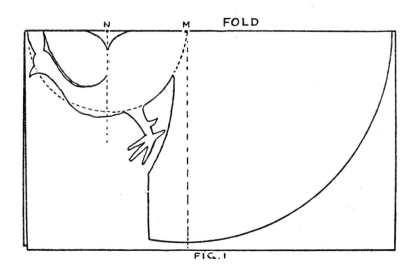

FIG. 1

Fig. 1. Fold a piece of strong paper with the crease at the top. With the aid of a compass draw parts—as above—of two circles, the centre of the bigger circle at M; and the centre of the smaller half-circle being at N. Fold the paper to give you creases from N and M. These will be helpful when you draw the Peacock, as above. Cut the figure out along the plain lines.

Fig. 2. Cut slits, like this, to make feathers on the wings and the tail. Take a good look at portion *a*. Four or five slits should be made in this.

FIG. 2

FIG. 3

Fig. 3. Unfold your paper, and lay it down flat. First look carefully at the above drawing. Just below A you will see some dotted lines. Using the blunt point of your scissors, and with the help of a ruler, press along these lines. Don't cut! Now cut down from B to A.

Fig. 4. Brush paste on the inner front halves of your Peacock, that is, the portions shown shaded at *a*, and stick these front parts together. Now push the side wings backwards, separate the head feathers a little, and pull the Peacock's feet somewhat apart.

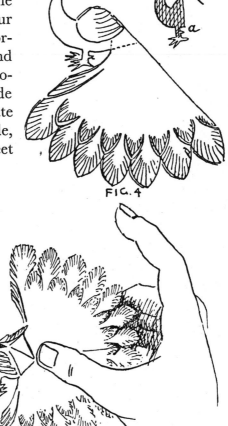

FIG. 4

FIG. 5

Fig. 5. Folding on the lines made with the blunt point of your scissors, bend the Peacock's tail upwards.

FIG. 6

Fig. 6. To stop the Peacock from falling backwards you now make use of the two portions *a* in Fig. 2 on page 118. Pull them backwards like this.

FIG. 7

Fig. 7. Turn the bird round to face you, like this. Your Peacock with feathery tail, is now ready for painting. The brightest greens and blues in your paint-box, please!

THE PUZZLE OF THE WELLINGTON BOOTS

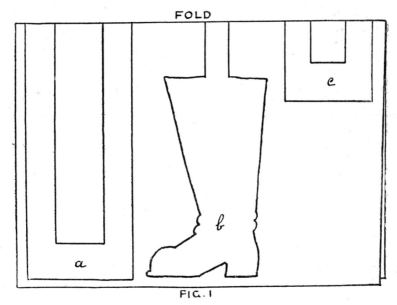

FIG. 1

Fig. 1. Fold a piece of strong paper in two, with the crease at the top. Draw and cut out the three parts of the puzzle, as shown. Keep part *c* fairly small.

Fig. 2. Unfold part *c* and place it over part *a* (still folded) as in P. Now, holding both sideways, as in Q tuck one boot inside the strip so that both boots hang down, as shown in drawing.

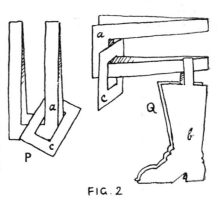

FIG. 2

121

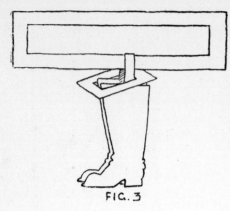

FIG. 3

Fig. 3. Now slide part *c* on top of the boots, like this. Unfold part *a* entirely. Ask your friends to try and get the Wellingtons off, without breaking the paper. This will make them scratch their heads.

CHAIN OF BEADS

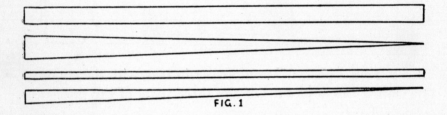

FIG. 1

Fig. 1. Beads can be made from very narrow strips of paper shaped like those above. Coloured paper—not too thick—will give the best results.

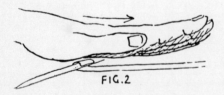

FIG. 2

Fig. 2. Use a thin knitting needle to roll up a narrow strip of paper, like this. Stick the loose end of the strip with paste, and then slip the bead off the knitting needle.

Fig. 3. By varying the size and shape of your strips of coloured paper, you can easily make beads like these. And they are only a few of the possible sorts.

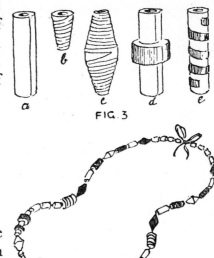

FIG. 3

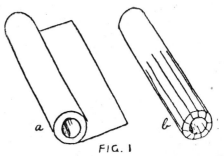

FIG. 4

Fig. 4. When you have made enough beads, thread them together like this—and you have a nice Chain or Necklace.

PAPER FLOWERS

Fig. 1. Take a long strip of coloured paper and roll it up as at *a*. Paste the loose end, so that it does not unroll. In one end cut slits up, as in *b*.

FIG. I

a

b

c

d

FIG. 2

Fig. 2. Flatten out the slitted portions and turn upside down, as in *a*.

Make a round stopper (like *b*) and push the point gently into the hole in the middle of the flower (see *c*).

Now take a narrow strip of green paper. Paste one end on the short stump below the flower. Start twisting the strip round and round, each time a little more downwards—spiral fashion. (See Fig. 4b on page 96.)

Lots of leaves can be made, in one go, by folding a piece of paper in pleats, as in *d*. Draw the shape of a half-leaf on the top fold and then cut out. Flatten out the leaves, which can then be worked into the spiral folds of the stem, as at *c*.

For the final result see Fig. 7 on page 127.

124

Fig. 3. For this type of flower, first make a stem from a long narrow strip of green paper. Roll it spiral-wise, as in *a*. Cut out several flowers shaped like *b*. For hearts, paste small circles like *c* in the centres of the flowers. On the back, paste one end of a narrow strip of green paper, as at *d*. Tuck the other end of the little green strips into the main spiral stem to form clusters (as shown in Fig. 7 on page 127).

FIG. 3

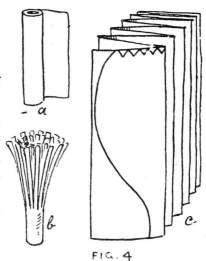

FIG. 4

Fig. 4. For a third type of flower first make the *stamens*. Roll up a strip of paper, as in *a*, and stick the loose end with paste. Cut slits down from the top, as at *b*. These are the stamens. Now fold another piece of paper in pleats, as in *c*, and cut out petals, as shown.

125

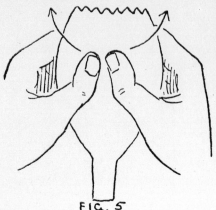

FIG. 5

Fig. 5. Unfold each petal and make a curve in each, by holding it like this, and letting your thumbs glide in the direction of the arrows.

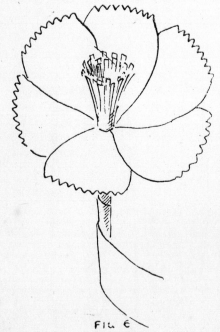

FIG. 6

Fig. 6. Stick the straight lower ends of a number of petals round the bottom part of your stamen shape (Fig. 4b) so that your flower looks like this. Now paste one end of another longer strip of narrow green paper round the stump beneath your flower, and then carry on as before, twisting the green strip spiral-wise downwards to form the main stalk. If you like, you can insert leaves in your spiral.

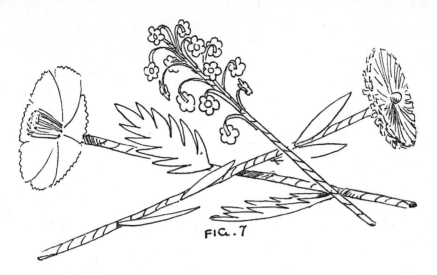

Fig. 7. Here are samples of flowers, leaves and stalks. You can improve on these, of course.

THREE MAGIC RINGS

Fig. 1. Take three strips of paper measuring 100 × 2 cm. Paste the ends of the first strip together to make a ring like *a*. Before pasting together the ends to make your second ring, give one end of the strip half a twist, as in *b*. Before making your third ring, give one end a full twist, as in *c*. Check your rings to make sure they look exactly like the ones drawn here.

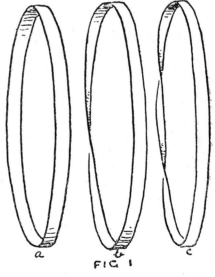

FIG 2

Fig. 2. Cut ring *a* in two lengthways. You will get two narrow rings, each 1 cm. in width (see *d*). Now cut ring *b* in the same way. This time you get a ring 1 cm. wide, *but* twice as big round (see *e*). Finally, cut ring *c* in the same manner. This is even more magical, for this time you get two rings, each 1 cm. wide, linked together as at *f*.

DOLLS AND DRESSES

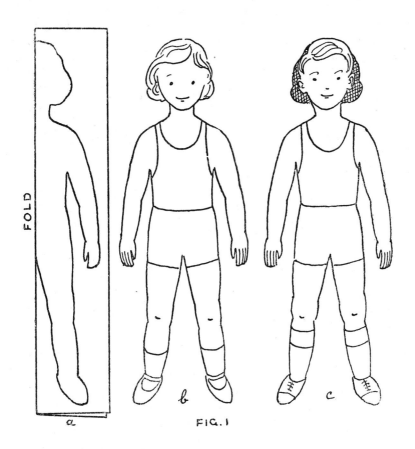

FIG. 1

Fig. 1. To make these Dolls you need cardboard. Fold a piece in two so that the crease comes on the left. Draw the figure, as in *a*, and cut it out. Unfold, and smooth out the crease. Draw hair, fingers, socks, shoes, etc., of the little girl, as in *b*.

To make a little boy, do all this all over again. Cut off the shaded parts at top of *c*. When drawing you must, of course, give him boy's socks and hefty shoes.

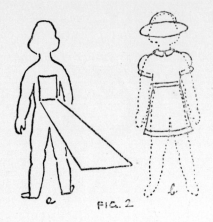

FIG. 2.

Fig. 2. The figures will stand if you separate the legs a little and fix a supporting piece at the back, as in *a*. To make clothes to size, lay your doll on a flat piece of paper (coloured, if you like) and then draw the clothes round it (as shown at *b*).

FIG. 3.

Fig. 3. To improve your outline you can now draw flowers and a ribbon on the hat; also frills on the sleeves and collar, fancy buttons in front, pleats—oh, you will soon think of all sorts of nice things.

On the shoulders you will need to draw two small strips, as shown. These, later, fasten the dress on the doll. Now cut out the hat and dress. Using sharp-pointed

130

scissors, slit open the hat where the dotted lines are drawn. Push the top of the doll's head through this slit.

Fig. 4. Hang the dress on the doll's shoulders and bend the strips backwards out of sight. Paste the strips down, if you think that better.

This hat and dress are only given as examples. You, of course, will be able to design far smarter hats and dresses.

FIG 4

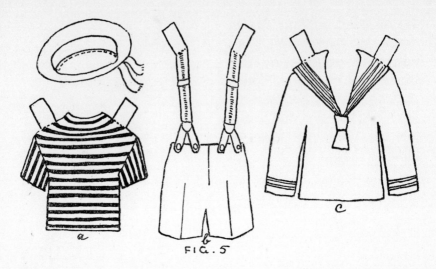

FIG. 5

Fig. 5. Here is a sample Sailor-suit for the little boy (Fig. 1*c* on p. 129). To get the size, first place the figure on the left side of your flat sheet of paper. Draw round it patterns of the jersey and hat. Then move your boy to the middle of the sheet and draw the trousers and braces. Finally, move him to the right side of the sheet and draw the blouse. Don't forget to add a pair of shoulder strips to all three garments.

Now draw stripes, buttons, collars, and tie, as above. Then cut out. Make a curved slit in the hat, along the dotted line at *a*.

Fig. 6. Bend all your shoulder strips backwards. First hang the trousers, by the braces, on the boy. Then put on his striped jersey, next his blouse, and lastly his hat. Now he looks a jolly Jack Tar.

FIG. 6

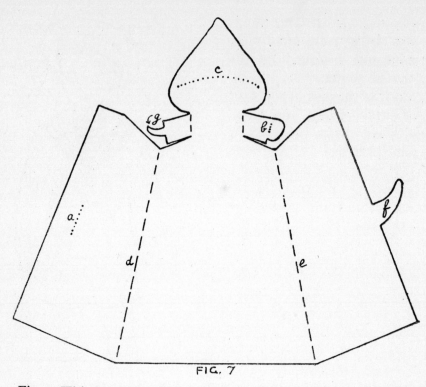

FIG. 7

Fig. 7. This boy's or girl's cape is made so that you can put it all round your Doll. Draw to pattern, and cut out the cape on the same lines as you did for Fig. 2 on p. 130. With sharp-pointed scissors, make slits in the cape along the dotted lines *a*, *b* and *c*.

Fig. 8. Lay the figure of the boy or girl on top of the cape and push the head into the slit made at *c*. Fold inward both sides of the cape along the dotted lines *d* and *e*. Push strip *f* into slit *a*. Now fold the collar round the neck, and push strip *g* into slit *b*. Finish by drawing buttons and pockets on the cape.

FIG. 8

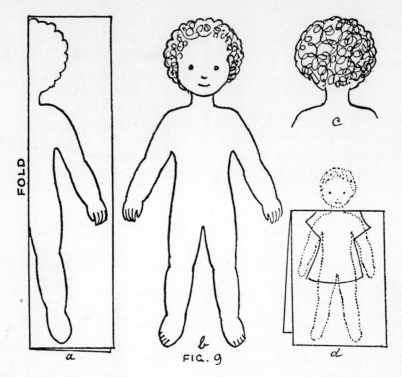

FOLD

a

b

FIG. 9

c

d

Fig. 9. Fold a piece of cardboard so that the crease comes at the left. Draw and cut out the figure at *e*. Then unfold and smooth your cardboard out flat. Now draw eyes, mouth, and hair, as in *b*. This baby Doll cannot stand on its own. So you must dress it back and front. First draw hair at the back of the head, as in *c*. To make the frock, take a piece of paper and fold it in two, with the crease at the top. Lay the Doll flat on the folded sheet so that the shoulders are in line with the top crease (see *d*). Now draw a frock pattern to size, as shown.

Fig. 10. This drawing gives a sample of a baby Doll's frock with sash or belt. You yourself can make all sorts of other frocks. When cutting out, don't forget to make slits at *a*, one on each side (to link the sash when folded round). There is also the curved neckline to cut away.

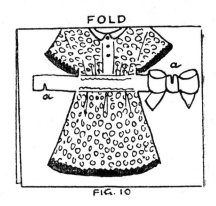

FOLD

FIG. 10

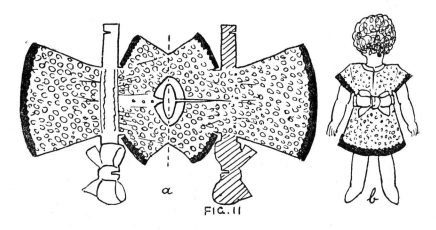

a

FIG. 11

b

Fig. 11. Unfold the frock, as in *a*. On the right, cut off the shaded parts of the sash (or belt). On this side, too, cut a slit from the neck to halfway-down the back of the frock. This will be the opening through which the doll's head will go. Now put the frock on your doll, sash in front. Fold the sash round the doll and fasten it at the back by linking the slits. The back should look like *b*.

137

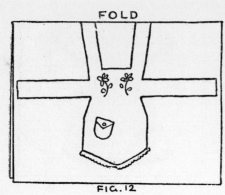

FIG. 12

Fig. 12. The Doll will sometimes need an apron to put over her nice frock. Here is an example of one sort of apron. Fold a piece of paper in two, so that the crease comes at the top, and then draw your apron. Cut it out in the same way as you did the frock.

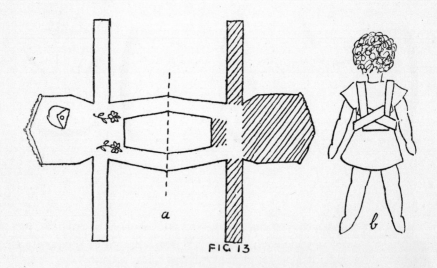

a

FIG 13

b

Fig. 13. Unfold the paper. Cut away the shaded parts at the right (see *a*). Hang the apron on the doll. Bend the side strips backwards and push them inside the upright straps at the back, as in *b*.

138

Fig. 14. This is the baby Doll in her frock and apron. Now, what about dressing her next time like a little Princess—or a Fairy?

FIG.14

139

FUNNY FACES

FIG. 1

Fig. 1. Fold a piece of strong paper in two, so that the crease comes at the top. Draw a funny face like this. In the *top* layer of your folded paper cut eyes and make a curved slit along the line of the mouth.

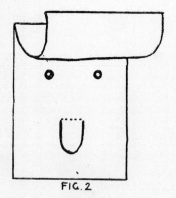

FIG. 2

Fig. 2. In the middle of the eyes, draw—on the *lower* layer of your folded paper—pupils, as shown. Now lift up the top layer of paper and cut along the (plain) line of the tongue. Folding along the dotted line, bend the tongue upwards a little.

Fig. 3. Push the tongue through the curved mouth slit, like this. Now, by holding the bottom corners of the folded paper and moving them about, you can make the eyes roll and the tongue waggle in the most amusing way.

FIG 3

Fig. 4. On a wide piece of paper, draw a funny face, as in *b*. Cut out holes for the eyes, as before, and make a curved slit for the mouth. Now curve the sides of the paper round to the back and paste the edges together. This gives the funny face a roundish look. Take another piece of paper—one that can easily be pushed up and down inside *b*. On this second piece draw two pupils for the eyes. Cut out a tongue in this piece, too, as before, and bend it upwards.

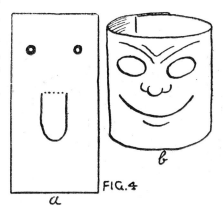

a   FIG.4   *b*

141

FIG. 5

Fig. 5. Push piece *a* inside *b*, and poke the tongue through the curved mouth-slit. Then, by moving the inner piece sideways, to and fro, you can make the round face look so funny that everyone will laugh.

FIG. 6

Fig. 6. Here are some more samples of queer faces. Can you draw even more comic ones? Try your hand at it!

JUMPING JACK

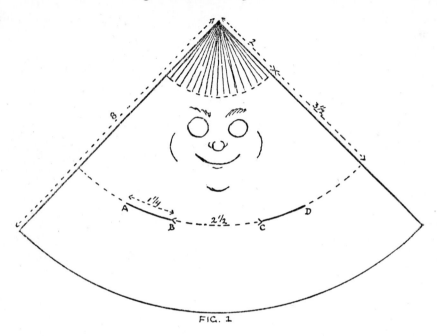

FIG. 1

Fig. 1. On strong paper draw a half-circle (with your compass) measuring 8 cm. from the centre. Cut it in half, and you get the above outline, on which you can draw this face. As before, cut out eyes and make a curved slit for the mouth. With your compass faintly draw a part-circle (see dotted lines) $5\frac{1}{2}$ cm. from the top. Carefully following the measurements in the drawing, cut slits from A to B and from C to D. Finally, cut lots of snips at the top, to about 2 cm. down. These make Jumping Jack's hair (see Fig. 6).

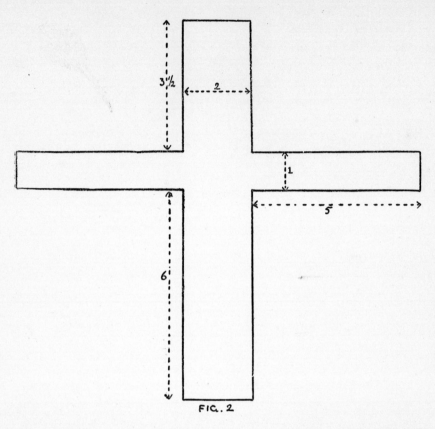

3¹/₂ 2 1 5 6

FIG. 2

Fig. 2. Using your ruler, draw the above design on a piece of strong paper. Note the measurements carefully. Cut out the figure.

Fig. 3. Lay the quarter-circle on top of the cross, like this. Mark the places for the tongue and the pupils of the eyes. Put the quarter-circle aside for a moment. Draw pupils on the cross. Cut out and bend up the tongue.

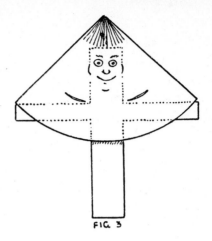

FIG. 3

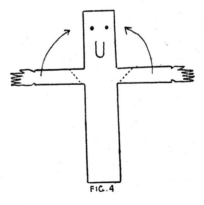

FIG. 4

Fig. 4. Cut fingers and thumbs in the cross-pieces, like this. Folding along the dotted lines, bend the arms inwards and upwards—as shown by arrows.

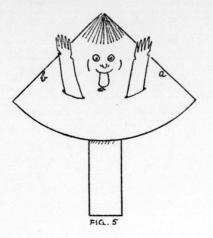

Fig. 5. Push the arms and tongue through the slits provided in the quarter-circle. Now curve sides *a* and *b* towards the back, and paste their edges firmly together.

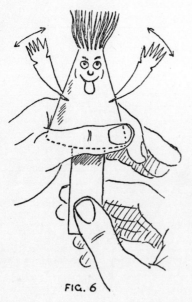

Fig. 6. Ruffle the hair at the top, and twist the arms sideways, like this. Hold Jumping Jack with one hand. With your other hand, move the inside piece about. Jack's arms will wave, his tongue will waggle, and his eyes roll.

146

CLIMBING SNAKE

Fig. 1. In the middle of a piece of strong paper draw the eye of your snake. With this as centre, draw a circle. Cut this out. Starting at the bottom, cut along the plain line which gradually curves into the centre.

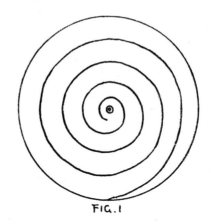

FIG. 1

Fig. 2. With the *blunt* end of a darning needle, make a dent at the back of the eye. Don't pierce it! Stick the pointed end of the needle into a cork, like this. Let the dent in the snake rest on the upright blunt end of the needle. Set it all in the steam from a small kettle for a few moments—and you will see the Snake curl round and down, just as though it were alive. Snakes alive!

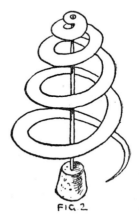

FIG. 2

147

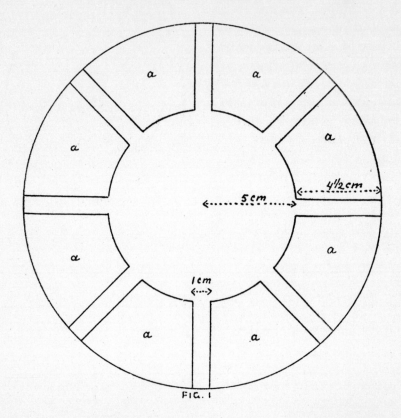

FIG. 1

Fig. 1. The drawing gives the measurements for making a very good Merry-go-Round. Using ruler and compass, carefully copy the above design on a piece of strong paper. The outer circle measures $9\frac{1}{2}$ cm. from the centre, and the inner circle 5 cm. from the same centre. The strips between the eight *a* parts all measure $4\frac{1}{2}$ cm. by 1 cm.

First cut out the big circle. Then cut out the eight *a* parts.

Fig. 2. On another piece of strong paper, draw a circle measuring 5½ cm. from the centre M. Cut out the circle. From A cut a slit sloping up to centre M. Brush paste on the part of the circle lying between points A, M, and B. Now raise the edge at A. Pull edge AM up (over sticky portion AMB) until it meets line MB. This will make the circle rise in the middle. Press the pasted part to make sure it sticks. This gently sloping cone is the Top of your Merry-go-Round.

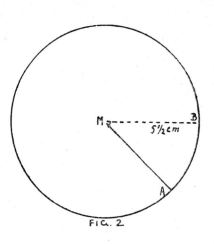

FIG. 2.

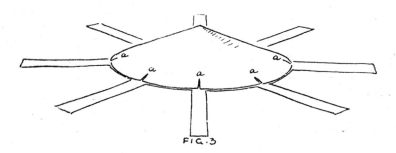

FIG. 3

Fig. 3. Lay the Top over the centre of your other shape, like this. Where the eight strips stick out, cut slits *a* in the edge of the top—making eight such slits in all. Now put the Top aside for the moment.

FIG. 4

Fig. 4. Draw, and cut out, eight little horses, like this. Take a look at Fig. 7 and you will see why strips beneath the horses are required. Bend up the part of the strips below the dotted line.

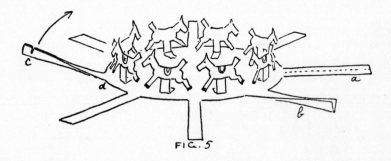

FIG. 5

Fig. 5. Stick the bent flat parts of the strips on your first shape so that each horse is near the edge and is halfway between two strips. Folding along the dotted line *a*, bend each strip as shown in *b*, folding it in two as far along as possible. Cut a little slit *c* near the top end of each strip. Folding at edge *d*, where the strips join the circle, bend all the strips upwards. Now fix on your Top by linking the slits in the strips with the slits you made (Fig. 3) in the Top.

Fig. 6. Fold two small pieces of paper in two, so that the crease comes on the left. Draw, and cut out flags, like these two. Cut slits at *a* near the bottom of the flag masts. You will need four of these flags.

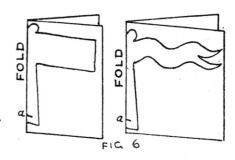

FIG. 6

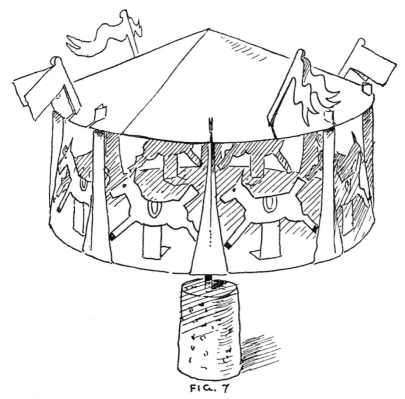

FIG. 7

Fig. 7. Make four slits in the edge of your Top—at equal distances from one another—and fit your flags in, linking the slits in the flagmasts with those in the Top. With a knitting needle pierce a hole in the centre of the bottom piece of your Merry-go-Round. Now take this needle and stick the pointed end firmly into a large cork, so that it stands upright. Slip your Merry-go-Round gently on the needle. The blunt end will go through the pierced hole. The Merry-go-Round will slide down until the blunt end of the needle is supporting the Top underneath its centre. Fig. 7 shows the Merry-go-Round—all ready to start.

REVOLVING MERRY-GO-ROUND

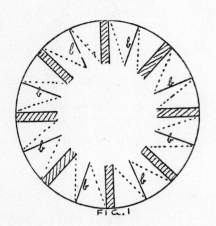

FIG. I

Fig. 1. Draw the bottom of this Merry-go-Round in the same way as shown in Fig. 1 on page 148. Cut out the big circle, but do not cut out, this time, the eight *a* parts. Instead, cut eight lots of *double slits* from the edge to the inner circle (to give you your eight strips, as before). Then cut—half-way between each of these strips— slits *b.* Fold your strips in two and bend them up- wards, as before. You now have sixteen flat pieces stick- ing out from the inner circle. Folding along the dotted line, fold each flat piece in two so that it will serve as a sail.

152

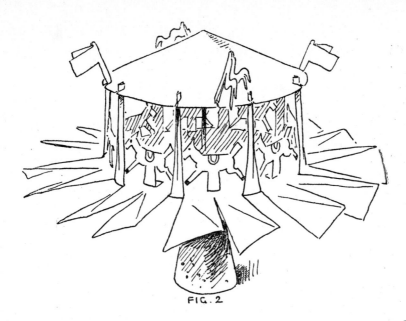

FIG. 2

Fig. 2. Now follow, step by step, the way shown on pp. 149 and 151 to make the Merry-go-Round. This one, when finished, should look like this. Blow against the sails, or just stand it where there is a draught or breeze—and round it will go, on its own.

ANOTHER MERRY-GO-ROUND

Fig. 1. On a piece of strong paper draw two circles. The big circle should measure 10 cm. from the centre M. The inner circle should measure 5 cm. from the same centre M. Cut out the big circle.

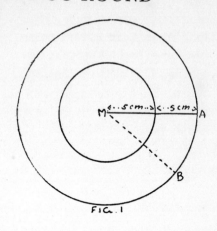

FIG. 1

From point A, at the edge, cut a line to the centre M. Brush paste all over the part between A, M, and B. Now pull edge AM over the sticky portion until it rests on line BM. Press it down so that the overlapping parts hold firmly together. As before (Fig. 2 on page 149), you will find that this has made the centre of your circle rise a little, forming a gently sloping cone.

Fig. 2. At equal distances from one another, cut slits *a* from the edge to the inner circle. Folding along the dotted line (as you did in Fig. 1 on page 152), bend the portions between the slits, so that they will serve as sails. This finishes the Top of your Merry-go-Round.

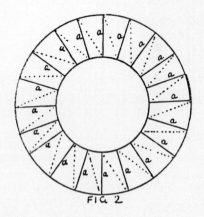

FIG 2

Fig. 3. Take a strip of paper measuring about 6 × 4 cm. Roll it up as in *a*, and paste the loose end to stop it unrolling. Cut slits at the top, as in *b*. Flatten out the slitted parts, as in *c*, and brush paste on them.

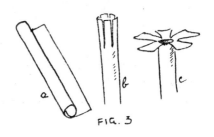

FIG. 3

Fig. 4. Set the roll upright and stick the pasted parts beneath the centre of your Top, like this.

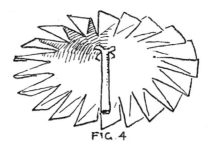

FIG. 4

FOLD
FIG. 5

Fig. 5. By means of long strips, you can hang all sorts of things on your Top. They are best made from coloured

paper. Take care to keep them light in weight, or your
Merry-go-Round will not easily go round.

The drawings in Fig. 5 give just a few samples of things—
aeroplanes, birds—which look well when flying round and
round. You make them by folding a sheet of paper in two,
with the crease at the *bottom*. Draw your figures, not forgetting
the strips leading up to the top edge. Then cut out. The
wings of aeroplanes and birds must, of course, be folded
along the dotted lines and bend outwards at each side. Cut
tiny snips in the wings of birds to make them look feathery.
Paste together the top ends of each pair of long strips.

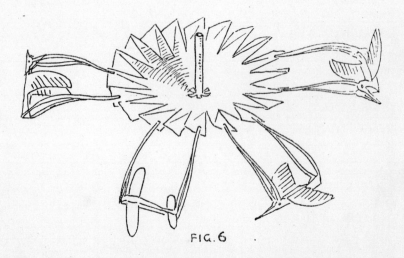

FIG. 6

Fig. 6. Paste the top ends of the strips underneath the Top, as.
shown. This drawing shows the Top upside-down.

FIG. 7

Fig. 7. Drive the pointed end of a knitting needle firmly into
a big cork. The other end fits inside the little roll (Fig. 4)
underneath the Top. Place it all upright. Now blow against
the sails, or put your Merry-go-Round in a draught or
breeze. And see your birds and aeroplane go zooming round
and round.